Additional Praise for
Get Momentum

"The first step of any new endeavor can be the most difficult. Too many options can leave you feeling demotivated. With *Get Momentum*, Jason and Jodi Womack distill their 20 years of experience into easily understood, action-oriented steps to simplify the process so you can not only get momentum for a new project or goal but bring it to fruition."

—KEITH FERRAZZI
Author of the number-one *New York Times* bestseller
Who's Got Your Back and *Never Eat Alone*

"In *Get Momentum*, Jason and Jodi lead us into a bright future, where stuck is the language of the past, and start is our battle cry for the future we envision."

—FRANCES R. HESSELBEIN
President and CEO of the Frances Hesselbein Leadership Institute and
1998 Presidential Medal of Freedom recipient

"Jason and Jodi Womack know how to *Get Momentum* and how to help others do the same! Their strategies are sound, their tactics achievable and practical and the results are amazing. I've been working with them for three years, and I've gotten two promotions, built an incredible team and am enjoying life at a whole new level. Don't wait, *Get Momentum* now and get started on your path to an even greater level of success."

—CHRISTI HARRIS
Vice President of Corporate Technology, Outerwall, Inc.

"Simple, effective, and a good recipe to get started. Womack powers activate!"

—CHRIS BROGAN
CEO, Owner Media Group

"The Womacks remind us that we are never going to be done—and then they give us a ton of great advice for dealing with that reality, maximizing our momentum, reaching key milestones, and making real progress on the things that matter most to us. Their advice is practical, actionable, accessible ... like all the best advice, something that we can all use right away and keep using. This book will give you a new way of thinking about the best paths to being successful."

—DAVID DEACON
Chief Talent Officer, MasterCard

"Jason and Jodi will guide you clearly, safely, and swiftly past the blocks that have kept you from sharing your best work with the world. If you are tired of feeling stuck, you need this book!"

—PAMELA SLIM
Author of *Body of Work*

"If you realized that a new time management method or a new smartphone app is simply not enough to be as productive as you would like to be, it's time for you to meet Jason and Jodi Womack."

—ANDREA ARESCA
Production Planner at Bestply srl, Italy

"I've been working with Jason and Jodi for years. They've helped me define and focus on what really matters in my life. Not only am I reaching my goals faster with their help, I'm defining very carefully exactly what those goals should be. More than once, I've drawn on what I've learned from them so I can get started when I'm stuck."

—Dr. ART CARDEN
Economics Professor, Samford University

"When you allow this bright yellow book to speak more loudly than the bright yellow sticky notes on your desk, you'll get momentum on the things that matter most."

—DAN LLOYD
Director of Business Development Information Systems, Allegro MicroSystems, LLC

"As a writer, I've spent more time staring at that damn blank first page than I care to admit. So the concept of being stuck is one with which I'm very familiar. Thanks to Jodi and Jason, I now have the tools to get momentum and move forward more easily."

—DAVE HACKEL
Network Television Writer/Producer

"I give bonus gold stars to Jason and Jodi for developing a master work that takes into account different learning styles and ways of being. They offer us options we didn't know were there."

—DYANA VALENTINE
Creator of SuperConditions

"We all get stuck. Jason and Jodi know that the secret is how you respond when you're stuck. This book provides practical methods to get your energy and thoughts aligned, so you can move forward with clarity and focus. It's all about building momentum that drives you closer to your goals, and creating habits that help you every day."

—DWAYNE MELANÇON
CTO, TripWire

"There are times when you know reading the directions makes it easier. *Get Momentum: How to Start When You're Stuck*... these are THE directions."

—IVOR SUBOTIC
Vice President of Global Sales, getAbstract

"As an entrepreneur, I am constantly performing a high wire balancing act while trying to juggle competing priorities. To get projects started and keep them from stalling you need to '*Get Momentum.*' Jason and Jodi Womack's latest book is a practical guide for those, like me, who need to motivate themselves and others to keep moving toward a shared goal."

—JON PETERS
CEO, AthenaOnline

"In their signature fashion of keen business savvy mixed with an entrepreneur's empathy, the Womacks lay down real talk that gets you real results. The best part? They walked the walk on everything in this book. Now stop reading my words, and get onto the really important ones Jodi and Jason wrote."

—KARA DEFRIAS
White House Presidential Innovation Fellow 2012

"*Get Momentum* is the must-read book from the team of Jason and Jodi Womack. Their commonsense step-by-step approach delivers the real-world proven tools you need to live your best, most truly meaningful life filled with achievement in the areas that matter most to you—your work, family, and life. Be ready to roll up your sleeves and transform your world with their practical guidance."

—TORRY BURDICK
Senior Vice President, Product Marketing, Vantage Production, LLC

"Getting stuck happens by chance, but staying stuck is a matter of choice. If you're ready to move forward and escape from a rut of uncertainty about where your life is going, this is the book for you."

—MARTIN JONES
Digital Marketing Leader, Strategist, Speaker

"Jason and Jodi's advice gets to the beautiful simplicity of personal success: Stop doing what used to work, get unstuck and build the momentum necessary to win!"

—MARC EFFRON
Author, *One Page Talent Management*

"*Get Momentum* is the most practical and powerful book I have seen about making progress at work, at home, or in the community. It provides a straightforward, proven approach through the Five Stages of Momentum and I will make it a must-read book for my leaders and colleagues."

—STEINAR HJELLE
Senior Director, Global Talent Development, Micron Technology, Inc.

"Jodi and Jason Womack bring together a combination of credible data and world tested wisdom to provide practical and actionable steps to break through whatever may be holding you back. An inspirational and informative read, not only for those seeking fresh momentum, but for anyone interested in a deeper understanding of motivation and the role it plays in our behavior every day."

—MIRIAM ORT
Head of HR, PepsiCo

"*Get Momentum* provides clear, practical advice to help you break through the bonds of the inertia that is holding you back from achieving your potential. These principles helped me take a product line with a decade of incremental improvements and transform it to a contemporary solution by breaking through the status quo."

—PETER S. MAHONEY
Senior Vice President, Dragon | Nuance

"Jason and Jodi are living the Get Momentum principles every moment of their lives and now gifting all of us with the tools we can really use every day to get out of our life ruts, the big ones and the not so big. Thank you both for the willingness to share!"

—JACQUI BURGE
Bossy, desk yogi

"Jason and Jodi are an unstoppable force. If I can pick up my game just 10 percent being in their orbit anything is possible. This book provides an opportunity to internalize their own experience and for each of us to be more unstoppable in turn."

—PIP COBURN
Principal, Coburn Ventures

"Jason and Jodi have helped hundreds of entrepreneurs get momentum on projects that matter most to them. They have captured the best of their insights on the topic in this gem of a book. If you are pursuing bold goals and want to reach them faster, this is a must-read."

—RAJESH SETTY
Cofounder, Audvisor and several other technology companies, and Author of
Gratitude and 15 other books

"Big companies, successful professionals, and even athletes—all have one thing in common. They had a starting point. *Get Momentum* is your ultimate guide to building processes, systems, and confidence to build a better business and be a better person."

—RAMON RAY
Publisher, *Smart Hustle* magazine

"Jason and Jodi have more momentum than any pair I have ever known. When you read their books or work with them directly, it's their accessibility that sets them apart. You realize your momentum gives them theirs. True to form, in *Get Momentum*, they're right here with you, giving you everything they have."

—RANDY HARWARD
Vice President of Material Innovation, Under Armour Inc.

"Reads like a handbook for creating great influence … The fast 'momentum' you'll get from this book forms the basis you need to expand your ability, execute effectively, and achieve success in business and life."

—RICHIE NORTON
Best-selling Author, *The Power of Starting Something Stupid*

"Jason and Jodi demystify that unspoken ingredient behind great accomplishment. They've captured their esteemed coaching format and made it available in this simple-to-follow book. Best of all, if you follow the exercises, you'll find your own momentum building with each chapter, guaranteed. As role models for momentum, Jason and Jodi in real life are the epitome of their subject."

—RICK KANTOR
MS creative catalyst

"Getting stuck? Needing to regain momentum around projects and initiatives that matter? Read *Get Momentum* and get back on track fast."

—ROB BERNSHTEYN
CEO, Coupa

"I've said it before, and I'm going to say it again. Their work has helped me recognize that my 'work' is directly affected by whatever lens (or lenses) I'm viewing my life through. And through their work I've been able to gain focus on maintaining and using the proper lens for the proper task."

—RYAN R SPEED
Cofounder and Head Coach, IRONWill HQ

"*Get Momentum* is a straightforward approach to not only self-improvement, but improvement of everything you come in contact with."

—SARA CHILDERS
Founder, Bare Philanthropy LLC

"Jason and Jodi Womack are two people who talk the talk and walk the walk. The elements in this book come from their years of experience, which I have witnessed, via webinars, 200 podcasts, over 200 YouTube videos and easily over 100 articles. The highlight was when I met Jason and Jodi at one of Jason's Coffee Chats. They were genuine and down-to-earth people who everyone gathered could relate to! They cared about all of the attendees and how they could help them get momentum to reach their chosen goals. *Your Best Just Got Better* was just the warm-up . . . . *Get Momentum* will give you leverage to not only reach the next level … it will catapult you even further!"

—SCOTT MOSKOWITZ
CPA, CGMA, Get Momentum founding member

"Everyday excellence is an opportunity for everyone who reads and uses this book."

—SHELLEY SHOEMAKER

"It's all about getting the momentum to continue to be a performer beyond an entrepreneur. It's easy to get stuck in entrepreneur mode vs. CEO mode. That transition is hard to make. Jason has allowed me to reset monthly and get focused on my Most Important Things, and I'm continuing to push to them."

—PAUL GIEROW
President, GATR Technologies

"*Get Momentum* teaches me to take smart action with a focused mind while satisfying the expectations of my heart."

—KRISTI PALMA
Development Editor and Writing Coach

"Hold on to your hat. *Get Momentum* is a fast-paced crash course in jump-starting then super-charging life ... even if you thought you were already rolling. This book is a gem, written by two people who have clearly done the work. It cuts right to the heart of the matter and leaves you feeling refreshed and rejuvenated. I see this book sitting at arm's reach from my work desk, as I know there will always be days that I need the reminder that Momentum is mine, if I want it."

—TONY UBERTACCIO
Business Coach to #SociallyConscious Mission Driven Leaders

"*Get Momentum* is a powerful must-read for both managers and senior executives alike."

—KATHRYN COX

"It is as if Jodi and Jason are right in front of me, coaching and supporting my efforts to be a better person."

—JOEL PASTORE
Director, Elevance Renewable Sciences

"What I love about the Womacks' book is how they artfully guide readers. Their approach is not overly prescriptive, nor is it woefully ambiguous. It's just right. They provide an expansive perspective that deepens one's self-awareness while empowering readers to take the best course of action for them. Simple, profound, inspiring, and tactical, anyone who puts forth the effort will surely Get Momentum as a result of reading this book!"

—ARIANA FRIEDLANDER
Founder, Rosabella Consulting, LLC

"Think of where you've been stuck in your life.... Now picture the exact opposite! This book has shifted the way I show up for myself, my family, my business, and in life."

—DEVON BANDISON
Founder and CEO, Devon Bandison Company

"Get the book, experience the personal tipping point, and move toward what you want moment by moment!"

—CICO RODRIGUEZ
President, Ingredient Sales Insights

"*Get Momentum* feels like a 'create your own adventure' book where you take an interactive front seat for it to be a wild ride."

—CLEMENS WAN

"Jason and Jodi Womack make getting unstuck part of your everyday plan and stop the W.U.T.W (what used to work) mindset. Jason and Jodi walk their talk and overdeliver on their commitment to their readers. Their ideas and lessons are invaluable to anyone who wants to plan and live a life of excellence. *Get Momentum* is a must-read for anyone looking to unlock your potential and truly Get Momentum in work, life, and family."

—STEVE HARDEN

"The Womacks move you forward; they don't let you stop, they focus you on what is new and what you must learn to continue. To me, their ideas are rays of sunshine, coming through the hazy cloudy sky; they make me see what I should have seen on my own but didn't. I don't know where I would be in this complex world of the second decade of the twenty-first century without them."

—STEPHEN SILVERMAN
Cofounder, Silverman & Milligan, LLP

"You've got to move forward toward your goals, but too often that's easier said than done. Jason and Jodi will show you how to get going—and keep going—with great insights, tried and true methods, and enthusiastic support. If you ever needed a polite but firm accountability partner with deep expertise to guide you, you may have just found not one, but two, in this new book."

—TOM CATALINI
Author, speaker, coach

"This book is the slap-in-the-face wake-up call that we all need. If you are stuck and ready to do what it takes to get what you desire in life, this book is for you. I just love the fresh keep-it-real approach that Jason and Jodi use. Jason and Jodi are a dynamic duo that has decades of experience helping people just like you get momentum. What are you waiting for? Get this book now!"

—GARY WARE
Personal Coach, Breakthrough Cocktail

"You hold in your hand a resource for leaders that goes beyond productivity and a business book of how-tos. This is a guide and encourager linked to a set of tools and a global community. Jason and Jodi will help you get unstuck and Get Momentum toward whatever area of life you have decided is most important to you, be it a new business, a new role, or a new set of leadership skills you'd like to acquire to improve your effectiveness."

—GREGG FAUCEGLIA
Chairman, Institute for Management Studies

"*Get Momentum* is brilliant in its power and simplicity. Jason and Jodi have unlocked something powerful because we all can get stuck. Their solution is simple yet brilliant, and following the steps they lay out in the book will change your life."

—HAROLD WIMBERLY
CEO, YGB Incubator

"If you're ready to stop dreaming and start acting in order to build lasting momentum in a specific area of your life, Jason and Jodi will help get you there. Read this book!"

—ANDREW DECURTIS
Philanthropist, New York City

"Jodi and Jason really do know the topic of momentum better than anyone I've read or know."

—BERT MAHONEY
Berchman.com

"Success is turning what you have been told is true into knowing what is true. This book does that."

—BRETT LAYMANCE

"When the Womacks write that the 'stuckness' you feel is temporary, it is a reason for hope. When they outline a five-stage model for making momentum happen, *Get Momentum* becomes a must-read. Jason and Jodi share with us what has helped people all around the world move from stuck to action."

—FRANK BUCK, EDD
Author of *Get Organized! Time Management for School Leaders*

"Momentum. It really is what we all need to be consistently and continuously successful. The Womacks are amazing coaches who understand human behavior and who can guide you from being productive to achieving the success you want through guided introspection. Their books and coaching programs will help you learn the habits and thought processes you need to maintain momentum in your life and career."

—JACKIE COMPTON
President, Balanced Equation

"Jason and Jodi have really cracked the code with their super-simple yet creative model to maintain a great work-life balance and achieve your goals. Get Momentum is full of excitement and inspirational stories that is going to get you started right away."

—JAPJOT SETHI
CEO, Gloopt

"Jason and Jodi continue to stun and amaze me with their collective ability to spark change and inspire progress. As a CEO and founder, my days present a never-ending series of challenges and opportunities. Having the ability to identify obstacles and sticking points has propelled our business forward."

—JOE BRUZZESE
CEO, Sprigeo.com

"Jason and Jodi Womack have written a must-have book for anyone looking to get unstuck, make their dream projects happen, and create sustainable positive energy in their life! The powerful strategies and insight shared in *Get Momentum* will benefit readers for a lifetime."

—KRISTI LING
Author of *Operation Happiness: The 3-Step Plan to Creating a Life of Lasting Joy, Abundant Energy, and Radical Bliss*

"One of the best ways to achieve ongoing success is to adopt a strategy that you can always turn to when you find yourself stuck. *Get Momentum* gives you the methodology and the tools you can use immediately to gain that traction and find your flow again. You'll definitely want to keep this book close so you can refer back to it over and over."

—KYMBERLEE WEIL
Speaking Strategist and Founder, Strategic Samurai

"I have worked with Jodi and Jason as consultants helping me organize my time, my life, and my work. Today I'm living my lifelong dream of helping people improve their lives. I promise that if you read this book your relationship with time and productivity will never be the same."

—LARRY CHAMBERS
Author, Adventurer, and Humanitarian

"Finally a no-BS approach to something business owners and entrepreneurs have been embarrassed and afraid to discuss, until now. What happens when you're stuck, and how do you get unstuck? *Get Momentum*'s practical real-life examples, and support network, will get you back on track faster than anything I've ever seen."

—LISA MACQUEEN
Cleaning Marketer and Cofounder, CleanCorp Australia

GET MOMENTUM

GET MOMENTUM

how to start

when you're stuck

JASON W. WOMACK
JODI WOMACK

WILEY

Published by John Wiley & Sons, Inc., Hoboken, New Jersey.
Published simultaneously in Canada.

For general information on our other products and services or for technical support, please contact our Customer Care Department within the United States at (800) 762-2974, outside the United States at (317) 572-3993 or fax (317) 572-4002.

Wiley also publishes its books in a variety of electronic formats. Some content that appears in print may not be available in electronic books. For more information about Wiley products, visit our website at www.wiley.com.

Library of Congress Cataloging-in-Publication Data:

Names: Womack, Jason W., 1972– author. | Womack, Jodi, 1971– author.
Title: Get momentum : how to start when you're stuck / Jason W. Womack, Jodi Womack.
Description: Hoboken : Wiley, 2016. | Includes index.
Identifiers: LCCN 2016008682 (print) | LCCN 2016014206 (ebook) |
    ISBN 9781119180265 (hardback) | ISBN 9781119180272 (ePDF) |
    ISBN 9781119180289 (ePub)
Subjects: LCSH: Leadership—Psychological aspects. | Self-actualization (Psychology) |
    Change (Psychology) | BISAC: BUSINESS & ECONOMICS / General.
Classification: LCC HD57.7 .W6556 2016 (print) | LCC HD57.7 (ebook) |
    DDC 650.1—dc23
LC record available at http://lccn.loc.gov/2016008682

COVER DESIGN: PAUL McCARTHY
COVER ART: (coil) GETTY IMAGES © JON SHIREMAN

Printed in the United States of America

10 9 8 7 6 5 4 3 2 1

To all Get Momentum members:

We are in awe of all the people who signed up for the Get Momentum program over the years, for raising their hand to the question: "Who wants to keep learning, growing and creating?"

You've showed up each month to keep getting better at what you do, enhance your skills, share your successes and ask yourselves: "What's next?"

You've pushed us to keep learning and growing along with you.

You've made us better at what we do. And we're grateful to have shared in your journey. Onward. . .

Jodi and Jason

Contents

GET
MOMENTUM

1

Being Stuck Sucks

Stuck Projects, Stuck Life

Is there something important you want to do? Maybe it's a career change you want to make, or a personal project you want to start. But for some reason, whatever it is, you haven't started yet. You're reading this book because you're stuck.

Consider us your coaches. For more than 20 years, we have traveled the world, working with people who are overwhelmed by the feeling of being stuck. We teach them how to get momentum. This book gives you the knowledge we've organized in a way that you can practice. These tactics work. We're not here to motivate you. There's more to it than that. We know you've heard inspiring clichés such as Nike's "Just do it" or "Leap and the net will appear" or "Think outside the box." Enough already!

Read this book, and you'll learn strategies that people around the world use to start important projects and achieve big goals, such as:

- Making a career change.
- Changing how their family interacts to create less stress and more joy.
- Training for a competitive athletic event.
- Starting a business to get out of a job they hate and into the work they love.
- Creating art.
- Planning an adventure on their bucket list.
- Losing weight and staying active for a healthier life.
- Transforming their retirement into the next vibrant chapter in their life.

We want to help you move from feeling stuck to getting started. Be bold and courageous as you complete all the Get Momentum Activities in this book. Each activity is designed to help you move forward.

This Thing Called Momentum

Think about the word *momentum*. What does it mean to you? If you had more of it, what would your life be like?

Momentum means you're moving, and things are happening. It means you're making progress, and it feels good! We will teach you a self-reflective process, a method for making the changes you want and starting the projects that are important to you.

For a moment, focus on what you'd like to start. Maybe you know what you need to do, but it's too big to even start. Perhaps you have so many things you need to do that you feel overwhelmed. Or, it could be a change you want to make, or a project you want to complete.

Next, we'll share with you what being stuck sounds, looks, and feels like.

What Does Being Stuck *Sound* Like?

We asked people around the world why they haven't gotten started. They want to start a project or make a change, but... There's always a "but."

Here are the top five things they say.

1. "I Don't Know"

"I don't know where to begin. I don't even know if it's possible to do what I want. I don't know what the result would look like. I don't know anyone who will guide me or hold me accountable."

2. "What I Have is Fine"

"Things aren't terrible. They always say, 'Don't fix what isn't broken.' I'll just do what I've always done. It (the job, relationship, or living situation) isn't *that* bad. I'll just keep on keeping on. If things change, they change."

3. "I've Failed Before"

"I tried to do something like this before, and it didn't work out. What's going to be different if I try again? Why should I keep working at it?"

4. "I'm Confused"

"I want something new, but that will undo some of the other things in my life. I'm not aligned with (my boss, partner, spouse, kids, etc.) on the changes yet. What if I make all these changes, and it's not better than what I've got now?"

5. "I'm Overwhelmed"

"This change I want to make is just too big and overwhelming. I'll never have the time it's going to take. I don't have the money to start it. I already have too much to do."

What Does Being Stuck *Look* Like?

On one typical coaching day, Jason looked across the client's desk in his office on the 37th floor. A long-time client, Stephen (not his real name) was a senior manager in a professional advisory firm in New York City. Looking out the window, Jason took in the view of blue skies over Lower Manhattan.

Stephen had been silent for about three minutes now, lunch untouched, his brow furrowed, his shoulders taut. The stress in the room was thick; Jason felt it, and waited. Why the silence? Jason had asked Stephen a question he had never answered out loud.

One look around the office and you'd assume Stephen had everything together: the Hermès tie around his neck, the dual 27-inch computer monitors side-by-side on his standing desk, the framed family vacation photos on the desk, and a painting of a fogged-in Pebble Beach golf course hanging on the wall. Stephen scheduled this one-on-one coaching session because he knew that Jason helped people manage the complexity of work-life issues.

To put it bluntly, Stephen was overwhelmed, stressed out, and stuck.

Stephen confided in Jason that he was about to accept a promotion, and he would fly to London every other Sunday and return home Wednesday. He would manage a group of 200 people, and his increase in compensation would be around 15 percent. This was the role he'd focused on for the past 18 months. But, Jason could tell something was off.

Before lunch, Stephen told Jason he had been diagnosed with hypertension earlier that month and still hadn't picked up his meds. His wife was worried, he said. He was spending more time in the office than last year. What's more, his kids had started visiting colleges; all three would graduate high school in the next five years.

After a brief chat about the local baseball team, Jason asked, "Stephen, is the work you'd be doing what you want to be known for?"

The question hung in the air through an uncomfortable pause. After a long silence, he replied, "Jason, it's what I've been working toward for more than a year. My boss knew it. My wife knew it. But, as I map it out, I realize how stressful it will be. How much of my kids' lives I'd miss. How much pressure I'd be under to, how can I say it, be in two places at once." Jason listened. Stephen went on.

"When I called you last month to set up our meeting, I thought I just needed to get more organized. The question you're asking me now, well, I just don't know."

And so began a year-long coaching program focused on just one Momentum Question that got the ball rolling. As Stephen's executive coach, Jason was not going to motivate his New York City client to make a snap decision or set up an ultimatum. Instead, he was going to help Stephen take the very same actions that you will practice as you read *Get Momentum: How to Start When You're Stuck.*

What Does Being Stuck *Feel* Like?

A trait among people we coach—entrepreneurs, founders, managers, senior executives—is that they continue doing WUTW (what used to work). During a phone call with Jerry (not his real name), a two-year member of our Get Momentum Leadership Academy, he said, "Last year, I started going in to the office Saturday mornings once a month just to catch up."

He continued, "Even though I know times have changed, and my role is different, it's necessary to work on the weekends. Honestly, I don't see any other way. Here's the problem: For the past three months, I've been going in every Saturday."

It had been 21 months since Jerry accepted this position at a new company. He and his wife, had moved from Northern California to Washington, D.C. He was leading a new team of developers, the work was exciting, and the problems he was solving were challenging in a good way. While in D.C., they had their first baby at the same time that his client coverage increased. And, with the work he was doing and his incredible production, he had just earned a much higher bonus.

Naturally, that eased some of the financial pressure Jerry and his wife were feeling. But, he felt stuck. His only response to getting more work done was working longer hours and seeing his wife and baby girl even less.

Our mentor, best-selling author and internationally known leadership coach Marshall Goldsmith—who wrote the book *What Got You Here, Won't Get You There*—wrote an e-mail to Jason and said, "Most people, especially those who are already successful, believe that because they do a certain behavior that has led to success in the past, the same behavior will lead to success in the future. I call this the *Success Delusion*."

We've all done that. You *used to be* able to pull an all-nighter. You *used to stay* out late with clients. You *used to work* through the weekend. You *used to catch* up on all your work sitting on a plane, or staying up late, or getting to the office early in the morning, or working into the night after your family went sleep.

That was then. This is now. You can't run your life based on what used to work.

Life Changes. Do You?

By now, you're getting a clearer picture of how you're stuck. You wish you could do more, do better, and get more done. But wishing things were different isn't enough to make things change.

It's human nature to wish ... hoping that things will be different later, that you'll have more time, and you'll be able to do what you want to do. You have to be careful. All that hoping might turn into resentment, or even regret, later on.

If you agree, it's time to do things differently. It's time to change. To *get* something different, you have to *do* something different.

Consider us your coaches. Naturally, we have our own personalities, and often, clients find the dual-perspective useful—kind of a "he said/she said." When you have a question about momentum, we're right here with you. Keep reading this book, and of course, you're free to join us online at www.GetMomentum.com/book so that we can provide you with the support you need to get unstuck.

As you get momentum, you will improve your leadership skills, learn to prioritize effectively, think creatively, and focus on the actions and tactics you can use to get more of what you want in life and at work.

We know that getting momentum is simple, but it isn't easy. You're the one who has to do the work. What we ask you to do will take time, energy, and focus. We'd like to forewarn you: There is a high likelihood that you'll need to stop doing some things that you've always done in order to get new results.

You're going to have to slow down to a crawl so you can stand back up and sprint.

The Power of Momentum

Now you know what being stuck looks, sounds, and feels like. So, what is *momentum*? Momentum is power. When you get momentum, you:

- Know that what you're doing is what you're meant to do.
- Know you have people you can trust.
- Feel accomplished at the end of almost every day.
- Have time to do what you have to do, so you can do what you want to do.
- Make significant progress on meaningful goals.

Prevent Regret

"I wish I had worked more," isn't what people say on their deathbed. Instead, people's dying wish is for more meaningful time with loved ones. Author Bronnie Ware wrote *The Top Five Regrets of the Dying—A Life Transformed by the Dearly Departing* after spending time caring for dying people in their homes. Review her list because you don't want to look back on your life and have any of these regrets.

1. I wish I'd had the courage to live a life true to myself, not the life others expected of me.
2. I wish I didn't work so hard.
3. I wish I'd had the courage to express my feelings.
4. I wish I had stayed in touch with my friends.
5. I wish that I had let myself be happier.

People tell us they're stuck on projects that are personal in nature. They want to do something creative like write a book or pursue photography. These projects get put on the "nonessential" list. Yet, these projects are essential to people's happiness and well-being. They tap into the core of the regrets listed above, because they are an expression of people's true selves. However, since these projects do not have an external deadline or immediate financial reward, they don't get prioritized. They linger in the limbo of "someday."

What Is *Really* Stopping *You*?

What is really in your way? Regularly, we return phone calls and reply to e-mails from people from around the world as they ask us to help them with ideas they can use to get momentum on projects that are stuck. Often, they tell us they want to get momentum, but everything they've tried hasn't worked.

Whether the goal is to be more engaged at work, be more present with your family, or start a side project that has stalled, the Five Stages of Momentum will help you get started, get momentum, and achieve more than you ever thought possible. When you approach that project using our step-by-step methodology, you'll create the conditions necessary to experience more success, easier and more efficiently. We're both fans of "process." And, even though sometimes it means that things take a little longer than planned, the changes we make are sustained over time.

Let the Get Momentum Activities we provide guide you to eliminate the reasons (excuses) you have had for not getting going. Among the circumstances we help our clients handle, here are three of the more common things we hear them say. As you read through each, ask yourself, "Does this apply to me?"

1. The People Who Offered Support Aren't Showing Up for You

Do you ever look around at how other people seem to have all the support they need? The support you don't have? Maybe a colleague promised he would help. Maybe your friends and family are telling you that your project sounds like a million-dollar idea. Maybe you've even had people promise they would order your product as soon as you're ready. Whatever the scenario, you've lost momentum because a part of you is worried that those who have promised to show up for you might not actually do it.

2. You're Getting Information—Just Too Much at the Wrong Time

How many business magazine subscriptions do you have? How many local business networking meetings do you attend each month? How many websites, news feeds, and e-books have you collected in your digital ecosystem—all with good ideas and promises that if you'll just do such and such, then you'll succeed?

3. You're Striving for Perfect Work-Life Balance

We've seen parents not ready to parent, students not ready to study, and managers not ready to manage. To get momentum, you need to understand what we mean by that. We know that it's a multifront effort. As you're working to improve things in business, you're also working to improve them at home.

Like many people reading this book, you're going to realize that simultaneously you want to:

- Empower your team so you can rise to your next level.
- Heal a broken relationship.
- Stay engaged with your life and work.
- Be a positive influence to your children.
- Nourish your body and your mind.
- Take your business to a whole new level.

You get it, right? Your mindset can be telling you that you *can* have it all, that you *should* achieve work-life balance.

But that's not how it really works. You may make a mess of what's been normal around your house or office for a while. You may really upset the people around you who have gotten used to you putting their priorities above your own.

You need to understand:

- There isn't some magical state called "work-life balance."
- Things won't be perfect with your partner every day.
- The friends you hang out with may not support the "new you."
- Your kids won't like you some days.

GET MOMENTUM ACTIVITY #1: What Does Being Stuck Mean to You?

Throughout this book, we'll invite you to participate in your own Get Momentum process by completing activities we've come up with for each stage of the process. In every chapter of *Get Momentum: How to Start When You're Stuck*, we'll ask you specific questions and suggest you answer those questions in a Momentum Journal.

Of course, you can hand-write your notes in a paper notebook, or use an app to type or audio/video record your responses, to each prompt. Please use whatever tool is most convenient for you. You can also download, print and share these activities: www.GetMomentum.com/book

Each activity is designed to help you understand your current situation, get started, and track your progress as you get unstuck. We recommend you (and everyone on your team reading this book) start writing in your very own Momentum Journal today. Keep this notebook or digital note-taking system nearby.

Are you ready for Momentum Activity #1? Here it is: Please open your Momentum Journal to a new page/note and record your answers to each of the questions below. This self-assessment will help you get in touch with your true goals, start getting organized, and begin working on that project that's stuck.

Plan to spend about 15 minutes on this activity, and be as honest with yourself as you're willing to be.

- What is the change you want to make or the project you want to start?
- How long has this been on your mind?
- Why start now? Really? Specifically? Why now?
- On a scale of 1–5 (1 being "most important"), how important is it that you get started? (That is, could it wait?)
- Describe what life will look like five years from now if you do *not* start now. Be specific and detailed.
- Why haven't you started this project yet? Make a list of all the excuses you can. (We suggest coming up with at least 10!)
- What are the old tactics (staying up late at night, working through weekends, etc.) you've been using to try to get started?

(*continued*)

■ Are you willing to spend a minimum of 30 minutes a day using methods you'll learn in this book to get momentum on the project that is stuck? If so, how can we help hold you accountable?

Ready? Visit www.GetMomentum.com/book to share what you're getting momentum on, and see what your fellow readers around the world are starting.

Nobody Does This Alone. Nobody.

The top performers in the world—athletes, musicians, actors, and yes, business professionals—all have coaches. When you add a coach to your professional development plan, you are more likely to do the work, make changes, and achieve the results you want.

Here's a quote to consider by Helen Keller, "Alone we can do so little, together we can do so much." Think about who you want on your team as you finally make the commitment to do the work to start that project that is stuck. Reach out to them today!

Keep reading and do the Get Momentum Activities. There's no theory, no fluff, and no "this-is-what-we-heard-works" in this book. We have done every activity we ask you to do. We've facilitated workshops and online webinars for more than 15 years using these very activities. We also facilitate these activities with members in the Get Momentum Leadership Academy. You are not alone. People around the world are using this information to get momentum.

You Have Our Support

Our intention is to help you be more productive and to make it easier for you to achieve your most important goals. We measure our success by reading your stories. Let us know how it goes!

Visit www.GetMomentum.com/book to gain immediate and free access to more than 50 resources, such as video lessons, expert interviews, research reports, and downloadable worksheets you can use as you're reading this book. Of course, you're free to sign up for Get Momentum Insights, our e-mail newsletter with ideas you can use to manage your time better, be more productive, and improve your work and your life.

For even more personal support as you're reading this book, e-mail us: Jodi@GetMomentum.com or Jason@GetMomentum .com.

To Do and Share

1. Decide that "now" is the time to get momentum on that change you want to make or project you want to start. Name it. Focus on it.
2. Get (buy, make, or set up) a Momentum Journal. Use it to document your ideas and progress as you read this book and complete the Momentum Activities.
3. Invite a group of colleagues at work or your partner at home to work through the five Momentum Questions together over the next five weeks.

Coming Up Next

Prepare to get momentum! In the next chapter we'll introduce you to the five Momentum Questions that you can use to get any project started. Go from hoping things will work out to following a reliable, step-by-step process to achieve your biggest goals.

2

The Five Stages of Momentum

Where You Are Now

Look, *really look*, at your life. Chances are things aren't all that bad. The problem isn't that you have a project you haven't started. The real problem is that your work *and* your life are pretty good.

Why is that a problem? "Good" can create conditions for feeling stuck. People who seek our coaching know that good enough isn't good enough. They want more. As Jim Collins wrote in his book *Good to Great*:

> Good is the enemy of great. And that is one of the key reasons why we have so little that becomes great.... Few people attain great lives, in large part because it is just so easy to settle for a good life.

By now you've tried to get organized and be more productive. Maybe you've hired a virtual assistant, downloaded apps to your phone to manage your to-do list, managed your personal time by

14

blocking your calendar, and even asked colleagues at work (or your spouse at home) to handle tasks you don't have time to do.

But you're still busy and not making progress on that big project that you've always wanted. It's time to change.

What We Know about You

After more than 15 years of facilitating workshops on personal productivity, project management, and effectiveness, we've recognized a requirement to getting momentum. Whether we're keynoting at an international conference for 45 minutes or working on-site with a group of executives through a two-day meeting, we know that momentum doesn't happen all at once. Nor does it happen just once. Consider the project you want to get momentum on.

As you think about the project you want to start, here is what we imagine is true for you.

You've Had This on Your Mind for a While Now

Here's the good news: You don't need to do a lot of thinking to decide what to focus on. You are reading this book because you have something you want to start or a change you want to make. Whether it's a work goal (starting a new career or business) or life goal (being more involved in your children's lives or taking on a community responsibility), that "something" you want to start has been on your mind for a while now.

You've Seen Someone Else Doing Something Like It

The more you do, the more you learn. People we work with have told us it was someone they met at a conference, a party, or while on vacation who inspired them to think something new was possible. Do you know of someone doing something similar to what you would like to do? Once you see or meet someone like that, it's tough to stop thinking about it. Now, we'll give you the tools you need to get going.

It helps to have an image in mind when you start something that has been stuck. What we can help you with—and this is *very* important—is balancing the comparison of your own results with what you perceive other people had to do to get to where they are.

Pick One—Just One—Project to Complete

In his book, *Your Best Just Got Better*, Jason wrote "Give yourself the gift of your own attention."

Perhaps you have something you'd like to start that has been on your mind for months, even years. This is not a "quick-change," "get-rich-now" type of program. The process we teach gives you tools you can use for the rest of your life.

We're going to ask a favor of you. Please, make a commitment early in the Get Momentum process *not* to try to get everything started all at once. This is really, really important. The late Steve Jobs said, "It's only by saying 'no' that you can concentrate on the things that are really important."

Throughout this book, we encourage you focus on just *one* project that you want to start. Then, once you get momentum and are well on your way to completing that one, you'll be in a great position to apply the Get Momentum process to other projects on your list.

We Are Here to Be of Service to You

When people see the title of our book they say, "Wow, I have a project that's stuck. Will your book help me?" We are confident that the tactics we teach in our workshops, online academy, and here in this book will work for anyone. We also know how difficult it can be to get started on a project that's stuck, especially one that's been on the back burner for some time now.

By applying the ideas—and doing the activities—in this book, you're putting yourself in the driver's seat of change. However, unlike a road trip, there is no final destination—just great experiences along the way that will make for great stories later on. The skills you'll practice in this book will apply to projects you have in your personal life as well as your professional career.

Note from Jason

Since 1994, I've walked onstage to speak in front of more than 50,000 people. Over the years, I've received more than 200,000 e-mails after coaching sessions, keynote speeches and seminars. I have personally coached hundreds of executives, entrepreneurs, and community leaders to get momentum in their work and in their lives. I won't say I've "seen it all," but I have seen a lot.

The most successful people I know keep learning. When I hear one of my mentors talking about one of her mentors, I realize—again—how important it is to discover and apply the very best practices and most useful advice.

Don't just read this book; complete every activity, and join the thousands of people worldwide who have started projects that were stuck.

Note from Jodi

When Jason and I cofounded the Get Momentum Leadership Academy, we knew that people like you would show up, do the work, and experience the wins. We had no idea, however, just how big it would get. After a speech I gave at the Women's International Network conference in Paris, women from all over the world told me things like:

> I always hoped my work would speak for itself. Now I realize that I have to speak up for what I want in my life.

> I always thought it was rude to ask for what I wanted. Now I realize that people can support me more when they know the goals I've set.

I was waiting. For what, I'm not quite sure. Now I know that to get momentum, I need to take action. And, you've given me the tools to do just that.

From 2009–2014, I organized monthly gatherings for women in business so that we could gather, talk about what we were working on, and ask for help from one another. During those five years and more than 60 events, I observed a few keys to success. I'm looking forward to sharing them with you in this book.

Now, at www.GetMomentum.com, we teach people how to progress on their goals by working with intention and focusing on their project for up to 30 minutes at a time. As you complete each Get Momentum Activity, you'll get momentum on a project that you've wanted to start—perhaps starting something that's been on your mind for years!

GET MOMENTUM ACTIVITY #2: Prepare to Get Momentum

Our job is to provide you with a clear and tested path that will help you every step of the way. We don't ask you to do "busy work," and we won't try to impress you with academic business philosophy.

Please open your Momentum Journal and review the three prompts below. Write down what comes to mind.

1. CLARIFY YOUR PRIORITIES

We believe this is a great place to start. Whether you're looking at your to-do list for tomorrow or planning the vacation of a lifetime, you have to know what's most important to you.

Stephen Covey, author of *The 7 Habits of Highly Effective People*, wrote, "The key is not to prioritize what's on your schedule, but to schedule your priorities."

Media mogul Oprah Winfrey said, "You can have it all. Just not all at once."

And, our mentor Frances Hesselbein noted, "Most of us will be remembered, in work and in life, for just a few words or deeds that made a difference to others."

Make a list of your current priorities.

2. BUILD YOUR CIRCLE OF INFLUENCE

If you change who you spend time with, you will change what you do, what you see, what you think, and what you believe is possible. Throughout this book, we ask you to consider—and sometimes reconsider—how much time you spend with certain people. The people you spend the most time with will influence you. And, you need to be careful. Some of the people you associate with can indeed increase the momentum you get on the project you want to start. Unfortunately, there are others who might not be so supportive.

The bigger the changes are that you want to make, the more important it is that you spend time with the right people. You want to find those who will encourage you, push you, and hold you accountable to your word. Every one of us has experienced the rush and the pressure of accomplishing something that we told someone else we would do. Had we committed this goal to only ourselves, we would probably have missed the deadline or dropped the project completely.

Make a list of your current circle of influence.

3. IMPROVE YOUR ENVIRONMENT

Change where you work and you change what you do. Improve your work environment or change it completely, and your productivity will soar. Within the next week, schedule a work session in a conference room, at your kitchen table, or at a local coffee shop nearby. While you're working in that new location, observe how you're more (or less!) productive, and watch what you do to get things done.

Make a list of where you work, think and create the best.

The Five Stages of Momentum

Next, we'll provide you with an overview of the Five Stages of Momentum. Each stage has one key question we want you to answer. Individually, you'll realize the questions are appropriate. When you answer all five of them, you'll realize the power of momentum.

Here's our promise to you: If you will pick *one* project and *only* work on that as you read this book, you'll do more than just get momentum...you could complete it once and for all!

Whatever it is that needs your attention, use the ideas and activities from one or more of the Five Stages of Momentum to make progress. Each stage offers you a strategic plan, complete with a Momentum Question to set the stage for getting started and staying focused, as well as specific activities to keep you on course.

Within one year of implementing the Five Stages of Momentum process, you'll be further along with your project than you ever thought possible.

Get Momentum Member Experience

Joe Bruzzese, founder and CEO of www.Sprigeo.com, wanted to change a part of his business for quite some time. He told us: "I had a great business, and it was growing. However, I was being pulled away from my family at night and on the weekends. I worked longer hours, thinking that at some point I would finally catch up. After several months, it became too much. I knew it was time to do things differently, but I didn't know where to start."

During a single Get Momentum coaching session one afternoon, followed by a month of follow-up phone calls, Joe completely overhauled two of his business processes: client acquisition and client retention. Within six months, he expanded his business even more, and he was spending more time with his family than he had the year before.

"The game-changer was going through the Five Stages of Momentum. The deeper we went, the more solid the foundation of my business became. But, it wasn't just that. I felt more in control than I ever had before," Joe said.

An Overview of the Five Stages of Momentum

Stage 1: Motivation

Momentum Question: What do I want to be known for?
By now, you know it's time to make a change. Maybe you're intrinsically motivated, you have something you've always wanted to do. Or, the motivation is extrinsic, someone in your community or a boss at work thinks you're the best one to start a project. Whatever it is, now is the time to get started.

Stage 2: Mentors

Momentum Question: Whom can I learn from?
Find a mentor. Work with a coach. If you're going to do something big that you've never done before, find someone who has experience and is willing to help you.

Stage 3: Milestones

Momentum Question: What are three subprojects I can complete?
The goal of momentum is to make consistent progress. Identify a very specific outcome or goal to achieve in the short-term (say, 3 months). We suggest you choose a series of small subprojects. Then, clearly identify the tasks, routines, and habits that will keep you moving toward the larger goal.

Stage 4: Monitor

Momentum Question: What positive things are happening that I can acknowledge?
Regularly assess your performance, productivity, and routines. Make a dashboard to track your actions and results. Stay on

course, and know (earlier!) when you're about to go off-course. Acknowledge what you and other people are doing right.

Stage 5: Modify

Momentum Question: What one change can I make to keep moving forward?
As you evaluate your progress, you'll see what is and isn't working for you. When you're not making progress, it's time to make a change. Of course you learn by doing, and as you modify your actions, you'll realize better and more efficient ways of doing things.

Do Something Different to Attain Something Different

This isn't another book on how to be more productive, and we're not going to ask you to do the same things that you've tried before, such as:

- Working later
- Waking up earlier

If you *want* something different, you're going to have to *do* something different. And the thing we want you to do differently is: *focus*.

Right now we ask you to pick the *one* thing you want to get momentum on. *Just one!* Now is your time.

As you read this book and do the activities we'll provide you with ideas and productivity secrets that teach you how to get more done, better than ever before.

We Invite You to Get Momentum

While the five-stage process may sound simple, the work isn't always easy. But we promise it's going to be worth it. If there's ever any doubt in your mind—or if your friends ask you if it's really worth it to do this Get Momentum process—just answer this question:

What will it cost me if I *don't* get momentum on the project that's stuck?

We believe that you can change your life by changing the information you let into your life. We are here for you every step of the way, and remember to visit the website www.GetMomentum .com/book for support materials and/or email us. Our goal here is to introduce you to the "rules" of momentum. Once you know how it works, you'll be able to apply this information to any and every project that comes your way.

Oh, one more thing: We wrote this book together because we belive in the power of partnership. We've been living, loving and working together since 1993, and we know that the book you're holding wouldn't look, sound, or feel as it does if only one of us wrote it.

Here's what we know, "Nobody Does This Alone. Nobody." Of course, we recommend reading this book with a friend or a group at work. By partnering, completing the activities and answering the Momentum Questions together, you will build a level of camaraderie and accountability that will make it easier to keep going even when the going gets tough.

To Do and Share

1. Review your list of priorities, identify the people who can help you get momentum, and set up a physical environment where you can be more productive.
2. Familiarize yourself with the Five Stages and Questions of Momentum.
3. Invite a colleague or accountability buddy to Get Momentum along with you.

Coming Up Next

Now you're ready to start Stage 1 of the Get Momentum process. You'll identify what motivates you to create results. Open your Momentum Journal to a new page, and get ready to answer Momentum Question #1.

FIVE STAGES OF MOMENTUM

Stage 1—Motivation
What do I want to be known for?

Stage 2—Mentors
Whom can I learn from?

Stage 3—Milestones
What are three subprojects I can complete?

Stage 4—Monitor
What positive things are happening that I can acknowledge?

Stage 5—Modify
What one change can I make to keep moving forward?

3

Motivation

We keep moving forward, opening new doors, and doing new things, because we're curious and curiosity keeps leading us down new paths.

—Walt Disney

People often say that motivation doesn't last. Well, neither does bathing. That's why we recommend it daily.

—Zig Ziglar

Perhaps I can find new ways to motivate them.

—Darth Vader

WHAT DO I WANT TO BE KNOWN FOR?

What Is Motivation, Really?

While drafting this chapter on his MacBook Pro, Jason looked up the word *motivation* in the dictionary app, which defined the word as "the reason or reasons one has for acting or behaving in a particular way."

Defining your core motivation makes it easier for you to decide what to do, and more important, to decide what *not* to do. Clarify several answers to the first Momentum Question: "What do I want to be known for?"

Now is the time to be ruthless about what gets your attention. Our goal for you is that you say yes to the projects that represent what you want to be known for. And, of course, to say no to the things that will only compete for your attention and get in the way of you getting momentum on the most important projects you're taking on.

Everything begins with some inciting incident—what you could call a motive for action. Think about a project that's stuck and identify specific reasons for starting that are compelling, promising, and significant.

Old-school motivation got you pumped up and excited but didn't always give you the tools to take action. As you continue reading, you'll see that *real* motivation is more subtle than you may have thought. When you know *why* you're doing what you do, it makes it easier to stay the course, do what needs to be done, and perhaps most important, know how to ask for help when you need it.

Your focus—not your time or money—is your *most valuable asset*. You need to be able to hold your focus on the answer to the question, "What do I want to be known for?" for longer than a moment, a day, or even a year. We're asking you to align with your legacy.

Being Motivated versus Getting Motivated

When we describe the Get Momentum Leadership Academy, the Get Momentum Retreat here in Ojai, and the workshops we facilitate for leaders around the world, it's easy to think we're "motivational speakers." We know you'll feel motivated answering the first Momentum Question. But, it's more than a fleeting feeling of inspiration.

We know real motivation comes from connecting to your purpose.

Think about why you do what you do. Instead of letting your to-do list determine what you work on, connect with what you want to be known for. Let this perspective guide your priorities. Do this now and you'll know why you're on the planet. When that happens, you can't help but feel motivated.

Being motivated is different from *getting* motivated.

We invite you to connect to the higher purpose inside of you. Let yourself clearly visualize—maybe for the first time in a long, long time—what you're really capable of, what you really want to be known for.

Although your answer to that first Momentum Question— "What do I want to be known for?"—may seem simple on the surface, the answers you write could keep you busy and working on more important things for the rest of your life.

GET MOMENTUM ACTIVITY #3: What Do You Want to Be Known For?

Open your Momentum Journal and answer the question: What do I want to be known for?

- List the names of specific projects you want to be a part of at work, at home, in your community, in the world.
- List an event you want to attend.
- List a community program you want to build or support.

Review your list. Okay, surely this isn't the first time you've had these thoughts and ideas. The more time you spend answering this question and the more you talk about it

(continued)

(continued)

with your friends and mentors, the more action you'll take in line with your purpose and the more motivated you'll feel.

It will take a trigger to feel motivated. Let this first question be the starting line. Committing to something you care about is a way to get momentum and keep on going. Just as it's easier to balance on a bicycle that is moving, it's easier to stay motivated once you are.

Where Do You Begin Getting Momentum?

When you slow down and give yourself the gift of your own attention, you might spot a pattern, have an epiphany, or see something that you'd missed before. After answering the first Momentum Question, people from around the world have sent us their insights. Here are two short stories members shared with us:

> It always felt like I didn't have enough. But, when I wrote my answer, I realized that I am already motivated. Not only that, I already have more than I need to get momentum on a change I want to make. I'm taking that 'not enough' energy I used to spend wishing things were different and directing it toward my volunteering position in the community.

> I realized that the work I am doing most days during the week really does inspire me to want to do my best. It feels like I promoted myself to a new level of engagement, just by realizing what I want my legacy to be.

Knowing "why" can even be more important than knowing "what to do." In 2009, Simon Sinek delivered a TED Talk titled "How Great Leaders Inspire Action," which has been viewed more than 21 million times at www.TED.com.

In the 13th minute of his talk, he said: "People don't buy what you do; they buy why you do it. What you do simply proves what you believe."

The question to ask yourself now is: "*What is motivating me to start the thing that is stuck?*" That is how you begin living your legacy today.

GET MOMENTUM ACTIVITY #4: When Are You Motivated?

Open your Momentum Journal and respond to the prompts below:

1. List at least 10 activities that make you feel motivated when you do them.
2. Think about times when you're so focused or you're having so much fun that you lose track of time. Maybe when you're at work solving an important problem. Perhaps in the car listening to your partner talk about his or her day. Or when you're out with your kids at dinner and you realize you're focused on what they are saying.
3. Highlight the activities that are directly related to the one change you'd like to make or one project you'd like to start.

Your Motive for Action Is Your Legacy

In his book *The 7 Habits of Highly Effective People*, Stephen Covey wrote about the four Ls of leadership: Live, Love, Laugh, and Leave a Legacy. The first Momentum Question asks you to consider the legacy you want to leave. "Why *are* you doing what you're doing, anyway?" Isn't that a great question?

How do you find out what *your* legacy is? Answer the first Momentum Question.

"What do I want to be known for?"

It may seem like an easy question to answer. You'll find that in pondering your answer, you'll realize there is more to it than you thought.

Take your time. You'll discover that as you answer the legacy question, you'll uncover a dual sense of urgency *and* energy that will push you along to the next stage of momentum.

The question is designed to get you to think about the bigger picture, because whatever you spend your time, money, and focus on now *is creating* your legacy. As you draft clear answers to this question, you may feel motivation like you've never had before.

But, you won't find motivation if you don't have a clear goal. Trust us on this. Without something out there you want (to improve, to create, to experience), everything will feel like just going through the motions. Set a goal and commit to getting started.

What *is* it that you want to get started? If you're ready to declare it publicly, visit www.GetMomentum.com/book and share your intention to get started. There, you can review and download support materials that will help you every step of the way.

Decide, clarify, and declare what you want to accomplish and you'll uncover the motivation you need to get started. Here are a few tips:

1. Make It Easy to See Where You're Going

Is the project you're starting on your bucket list? Is it a big one, something that you've dreamed of for a long, long time? In the words of Jim Collins, author of the book *From Good to Great*, it may be a "BHAG...a big, hairy, audacious goal." Spend more time in your Momentum Journal writing what achieving that goal will mean to you. Clarify the big "why."

Want to make it easier to believe that it's possible to live your legacy? Look for examples and read stories about people who have accomplished something like what you hope to achieve. The more you see other people succeeding and the more you learn about how they did it, the easier it is that you will believe your goal is both realistic and attainable.

2. Track Your Progress a Month at a Time

Keep a record of your progress. A daily journal entry or a weekly log can provide you with details about the process of progress. Monthly reviews can motivate you further as you can see how far you've come and how much you've accomplished. Reviewing your own notes can inspire you to keep pushing ahead. Seeing progress through time can trigger the feeling of motivation and inspiration that you'll need during the times when it seems challenging to continue.

Keep your Momentum Journal nearby, as you'll think of new ideas about that change you want to make or that project you want to start. You'll capture thoughts you have as you have them. Then, you can review and organize your ideas about achieving your goals.

Record and review as you go and you'll find that you're starting the project that was stuck. Often, simply writing something down can motivate you. Maybe you realize how far you've come and feel inspired to keep going. Or, you may recognize you still have a long way to go, but found a way to divide the work into smaller tasks you can complete.

3. Focus on the Feeling of Achievement

Be aware that at some intervals, you'll hit a slump. When that challenge comes, when you try and fail, when you give your all and come up short, remember to refocus on the bigger question: "What do I want to be known for?"

You know that saying "Out of sight, out of mind"? Well, it applies to the Get Momentum process as well. All too often, you achieve a goal and quickly move on to the next without pausing to reflect on success. Remind yourself regularly of success and you'll be even more motivated to magnify what you're doing.

The Psychology of Motivation

Two things drive you to change:

1. Some idea is inside of you that you just can't shake.
2. Something or someone encouraging you to take action.

We call these frameworks intrinsic motivation and extrinsic motivation, respectively. Understanding your relationship to each makes it easier to get momentum when you're stuck.

Intrinsic motivation addresses one of the factors that Daniel Pink, author of the book *Drive*, calls "autonomy." He says that the desire to direct our own lives is innate. "All of us want to be part of something bigger than ourselves, something that matters."

Later in this chapter, you'll read about Jodi's momentum experience of using her own intrinsic motivation to start the Women's Business Social at www.NoMoreNylons.com. She listened to what she said to herself, "Someone should host a networking event that women in business actually want to attend!" That was what it took to realize that *she* was the someone she had hoped would take action.

Extrinsic motivation comes in the form of change. A change in the economy, a promotion at work, an empty nest at home, a shake-up in the industry, or even a personal crisis. Any one of these factors can challenge you.

At some point in your life or career, someone has called and offered you a job or invited you to go on a trip. Has it ever happened that before they made the invitation, you didn't even know you wanted to do that thing? But there, in the moment that they asked, you were motivated to start *changing*, to take on the project *they* asked you to start.

Jason's Momentum Experience

In 2006, I realized that I was never going to be promoted to the senior management team at the consulting firm I worked with.

I could picture the next level of my career development, yet there was not a place—and never would be—for me there. I realized if things were going to be different, I would have to initiate that change.

Today, when someone asks, "Jason, how did you have the courage to leave a full-time job with benefits?" I smile and say, "My situation motivated me. I didn't have any other choice!"

Conflict and Motivation

Do you want to know what motivates you? It's easy: Identify where you have inner conflict. Think of something "out there" that makes you feel frustrated or even angry. Think about how things are, and imagine how you'd like them to be.

- Are you going to a job every day that makes you feel sick to your stomach?
- Do you argue with someone about old decisions that you can't do anything about now?
- Do you focus on maintaining goals that you're not able sustain anymore?

GET MOMENTUM ACTIVITY #5: What Frustrates You?

In your Momentum Journal, list five things you see regularly or deal with that frustrate you or make you feel conflicted. Be real here. Write real things: life things, work things, community things. Those "normal" everyday things might be the perfect place to notice you're motivated to take action and make things different.

When you're ready, write in your journal about how getting momentum on the change you want to make or the project you want to start will fix that problem or make things better for you, your work, your family, or your community.

Get Momentum Member Experience

Get Momentum member Ariana Friedlander told us about starting a project she'd been thinking about for a long time. Her ah-ha! moment came when she thought, "I want to build my legacy in a way that is authentic to who I am and what I want."

Within six months of starting her own business, Rosabella Consulting, in Fort Collins, Colorado, Ariana recognized a need to continue learning how to be an entrepreneur. It was critical if she was going to succeed.

So, she launched EntrepreNerds.biz, an accountability book club for her clients to implement the ideas from the great books she had been reading. Why? The more she read those leadership books, the more she found she could gain if she'd just apply what she learned. This was a way to create the support she and other entrepreneurs needed to apply new ideas to their businesses.

Their Why Isn't *Your* Why

We're assuming you have attended "motivational" presentations. Is the experience always the same? *During* the program, you listen to the inspirational stories and that makes you feel great! But, you are not sure how to take action with that positive energy when you return to your daily life. Yeah, we've been there too!

It can be a challenge to listen to someone who is already motivated. As they tell you what *they* did, how *they* did it, and why it was important to them, you may find yourself thinking something like, "But, that's not what I would do". Sure their effort was impressive—*they* faced hardships and overcame challenges—but *their* reasons were based on *their* motivation, *their* motives for action.

Maybe you listened to the story of a mountain climber who made it to the top of the world's highest peak, an Olympic gold-medal winner, or a local celebrity who made it through some adversity. Yes, they are amazing stories of what they accomplished. Maybe they talked about how they were raised to be resilient or had a life-changing experience that led them to achieving their goal. Those inspirational stories motivate an audience for a little while, but the enthusiasm you feel rarely lasts. Why? Their motives aren't yours, and there's no connection between feeling motivated and putting that to work for yourself.

The Get Momentum Leadership Academy

We launched the Get Momentum Leadership Academy in 2013 to continue working with people we served in our live workshops. We knew we could help them keep the momentum going by connecting their motivation to their actions if we were in contact more than just once. Really, we wanted to fix a problem: Companies, big and small alike, spend huge amounts of money each year on a single *big* meeting that brings in trainers like us to work with employees for a day, only to have those employees lose the enthusiasm (aka motivation) just days after the events.

So we changed our business model from just offering one time presentations to providing ongoing coaching to a global community of managers, executive directors, teachers, community leaders, and so many more.

Each month, we focus on a single leadership skill and publish a special report with assessments and activities.

Once a month, we produce an online global Master Class that dives in deep to that monthly skill.

And twice a month, we host a virtual #CoffeeChat conference call for members to call in and receive real-time coaching on the project they're working on.

As you've seen, we draw on our members' experience in using, testing, and learning from the same tactics you're practicing now. Here's another account of a member getting momentum.

Get Momentum Member Experience

Nicole Anthony wanted a better way for women to experience a more personalized online community. Her private social community, called L District (L = ladies), focuses on fun, quality of life, and relationships. When she thinks about what she wants to be known for, she is clear: to create a place where women can relate, collaborate, and uplift one another. That intention guides every decision the makes and everything she designs for the residents of her community.

GET MOMENTUM ACTIVITY #6: How Do You Spend Your Time?

In one of Jason's favorite books, *The Effective Executive*, Peter Drucker wrote an entire chapter titled "Know Thy Time," in which he recommends leaders track their time.

He said, "Everything requires time. It is the only truly universal condition. All work takes place in time and uses up time. Yet most people take for granted this unique, irreplaceable, and necessary resource. Nothing else, perhaps, distinguishes effective executives as much as their tender loving care of time."

In your Momentum Journal, experiment with answering the questions below to help you understand how you spend your time and to explore your motives for changing the way you do things.

- What do I spend my time doing?
  Keep a time log for a week. When you do this, you'll find out how much time you are (or are not) spending on your priorities.
- What do I spend my money on?
  Track your spending for a month, and you'll see where you're investing that limited resource. Is what you're buying on your list of priorities aligned with what you want to be known for?
- What do I wish were different?
  As you spend time answering this question, you'll realize there are deeper levels to what you're motivated to start.

- Do I really need to make changes now? Should and can I wait?

  Now it's time to commit to the process. If you're going to get started, you're going to have to make some changes. Are you ready? Really?

Commitment and Motivation

When you commit, you stand up for what you're doing and why you're doing it. By now, you're motivated to do what you promise to do. When that promise is to yourself, you'll feel ready—and inspired—to get started.

Take a moment and reflect on this quote by Johann Wolfgang Von Goethe:

> Until one is committed, there is hesitancy, the chance to draw back, always ineffectiveness. Concerning all acts of initiative and creation, there is one elementary truth, the ignorance of which kills countless ideas and splendid plans: that the moment one definitely commits oneself, then providence moves too.
>
> All sorts of things occur to help one that would never otherwise have occurred. A whole stream of events issues from the decision, raising in one's favor all manner of unforeseen incidents, meetings and material assistance which no man could have dreamed would have come his way. Whatever you can do or dream you can, begin it.
>
> Boldness has genius, power and magic in it. Begin it now.

Want to create even more momentum? Give someone your word. Tell a colleague, family member, or friend what you're going to do and when you'll share your progress. You don't need to commit to a final completion date; create an interim milestone to work toward that will get you going. This way, it's not just an idea in your head. This person is now counting on you. You will be more motivated with your word on the line.

You're the kind of person who keeps your word, right?

Beware of Momentum Saboteurs

Watch out for people who criticize your enthusiasm and accomplishments. This is sometimes referred to as "tall poppy syndrome," where anyone showing genuine merit gets cut down or attacked until they're back to "normal." In the East, they have a saying: "The nail that stands out gets hammered down." Interestingly, if you're outgoing, enthusiastic, and motivated to create the life you desire, you may be accused of:

- Having too much energy
- Working too much
- Trying too hard
- Never relaxing
- Always wanting more, never being satisfied

Don't let these accusations get to you. You're a creator, a maker, a doer. You look out and wonder (all the time) how things could be a little bit better. But, more than wonder, you wander. You get out, you meet new people, you try things, and you are making things better day by day.

Early in the process, start building your support system as people around you might do things to *demotivate* you from wanting to do, be, or have your best. The following four Stages of Momentum will equip you with resources you can use to overcome the saboteurs.

Jodi's Momentum Experience

I woke up one day with a realization. I thought, "Hey, I'm a business owner. Business owners go to networking events to meet other business owners. I should do that."

I went to a local business meeting. And another, and then another. There were so many different events I could go to each month if I wanted. But, after each one I only felt more lonely and more discouraged than before. This was in late 2008, a time when the economy was melting, and everyone had a story about how bad their business was.

Late one evening, on my way home from the last event I attended that year, I thought, "I'm glad I didn't go to one of these meetings before we started the company!"

Yet, I knew I had to get out into the business community. I would say, "Somebody should put together a fantastic networking event that people actually want to go to.

Somebody should figure out how to bring key people together, so we know all the great business resources in town."

Somebody should…

One morning over coffee with Jason, I was doing my "*Someone should…*" rant when Jason said, "Hey, Jodi, I actually think that 'somebody' is you. Schedule your own event next month, invite the business owners you know here in Ojai, and see what happens!"

I called the owner of a local restaurant and asked if she'd open the banquet room on a Tuesday night. My hope was she'd let me have it for free since it was a slow night. She said, "You can have it on one condition." I waited nervously as she continued: "You let my daughter and I attend whatever you're doing." Done deal!

I invited a dozen women business owners to join me for after-work drinks and conversation. Instead of asking everyone to introduce themselves and give the elevator pitch for their company, I asked each woman to share what she wished people knew about her as a person, as a family member, as a business owner, or as a community member.

The change in tone was immediate and powerful. People relaxed and talked vulnerably and conversationally. We laughed, joked, and actually got to know one another in the space of two hours.

A week later, I received several "thank you" calls and e-mails. Each person asked me about the next gathering. They wanted to bring friends. "Ah, the next one," I thought. "That's a great idea!"

The Women's Business Social went on each month for almost five years. I built a website (www.NoMoreNylons.com) and an online community. As I traveled with Jason, I hosted Socials in New York, London, Zurich, and other fabulous cities across the United States and Europe.

I called the group No More Nylons because it personified the kind of attitude we had about getting out of the work we *have to do* and into doing the work we *love*.

The Power of Momentum

Now that you're motivated: Own it. You are ready and willing to make progress on that "thing" you know needs to happen. Enough of saying, "Someone should do something about this. . . ." You accept that *you* are the person who should. *You* are the one to do something about the conflict you see going on out there.

You don't (necessarily) do it for the fame or the glory. You do it because it needs to be done. And, as far as you can tell, you're the one who views this as a problem to solve.

Make the commitment to yourself. Say, "This is it," and start taking action to become what you want to be known for. Do this, and you'll start noticing others around you who are also motivated. You'll see more people "living their why." Not in a "motivated" or "rah-rah" excited way. Many times, the most motivated and inspired people you talk to are the quiet, mindful, artistic ones that simply are. Motivated doesn't need to mean excited or energetic. It means you're engaged, you're powerful, you're committed to yourself.

Remember, the people in history who have made amazing things happen have not been the ones who stand by and watch. You realize that the people who make things happen are instead the ones who stand up and declare, "Enough is enough. I'm doing this."

To Do and Share

1. This isn't your parents' generation of motivation. You don't get motivated as much as you discover and clarify what frustrates you (a conflict that needs to be resolved) and what you've promised yourself and others you'll do (the commitment to act).
2. Stage 1 of Momentum is simple: You feel called to do something. Spend some time answering the legacy question: "What do you want to be known for?"
3. If you're not sure what you want to start, find something that bothers you. Attend a local community event. Sit in on a meeting with leaders from another department in your company. Subscribe to a magazine or read a nonfiction book about a topic that you're concerned about.

Coming Up Next

In the next chapter, you'll build on the momentum you're creating by talking with mentors about your BHAGs (big, hairy, audacious goals). These mentors will help you navigate obstacles and keep you going when all you want to do is quit.

FIVE STAGES OF MOMENTUM

Stage 1—Motivation
What do I want to be known for?

Stage 2—Mentors
Whom can I learn from?

Stage 3—Milestones
What are three subprojects I can complete?

Stage 4—Monitor
What positive things are happening that I can acknowledge?

Stage 5—Modify
What one change can I make to keep moving forward?

4

Mentors

Whenever I am asked what is the missing link between a promising businessperson and a successful one, mentoring comes to mind.
—Richard Branson

A mentor is someone who allows you to see the hope inside yourself.
—Oprah Winfrey

Adapt what is useful, reject what is useless, and add what is specifically your own.

—Bruce Lee

WHOM CAN I LEARN FROM?

What Is A Mentor, Really?

In nearly every organization we've served over the years, leaders tell us that mentoring is a key aspect of employees' professional development.

Think about what that word even means to you. According to the dictionary, a mentor is "an experienced person in a company, college or school who trains and counsels new employees or students." We define a mentor as, "Someone with experience you're looking to gain who is in a position to teach you what they know either in person, or through the work they've published and produced."

In this chapter, you'll clarify what mentoring means to you and learn how you could benefit by having a mentor help you get momentum on your projects, your career, and your life.

Review your answers to the first Momentum Question—"What do you want to be known for?"—and then ask, "Whom do I know that has something to teach me about that?"

Answer this Momentum Question and do the activities in this chapter to unlock potential you may not have known existed. We know that when you meet with a mentor you'll gain ideas, save time, and achieve more…often faster.

Find Your Mentors

Once you ask yourself the second Momentum Question—"Whom can I learn from?"—it is only natural to think of specific people who have influenced you.

Before we go on, let's refine a working definition of *mentor* to "a person with more experience in business or in life who can help you hone your abilities and skills, while helping you prepare for new opportunities."

Consider your teachers, coaches, managers, family members, and friends you've met over the years. Whatever the project is that you want to start, look for examples of people who have "walked the walk" and whom you can look to, learn from, and copy.

GET MOMENTUM ACTIVITY #7: Who Has Done Something You Now Want to Do?

Open a new page or note in your Momentum Journal.

Set a timer for 30 minutes and respond to this question: *Who do I already know whom I can talk with, interview, or otherwise learn from who have done something like what I want to do?*

One way to do this is to write about how your project is stuck. Identify the people you know who could help you get unstuck. Capture what you know about these people, what they did, how they may have learned what they know, and what they had to do to get to where they are.

The more information you gather now, the more you can refer to throughout your process of getting momentum and making progress on the project that's stuck.

The Function of Mentors

Great mentors help you get momentum. You'll benefit from regularly meeting with people who are willing to help you through their experience in both professional and personal ways. Just remember that your mentors are there to *support* you, not motivate you or do the work for you.

Before you continue reading, bring to mind a situation in your past when meeting with someone who had more experience than you helped you learn more and even save time. Now that you have someone (or a few people) in mind, consider the following purposes of meeting with mentors.

1. Mentors Help You Build Resilience

Sometimes we need to get out of our own heads. Sometimes we think we have it especially tough, and we forget to recognize that other people have had challenges as well. Many times when we sit down with a mentor to talk about a project that's giving us trouble, we hear a story from someone who had bigger problems than we did, and how they managed through it all. Hearing that they had it hard, and made it, helps us recommit to the work we need to do.

We also suggest you add studying biographies to your list of ways to build momentum. By reading about other people you'll see that they also had to deal with difficulty and challenge. Knowing how hard someone else worked to achieve their goals or dreams gives you an extra boost of confidence and resolve to stick with it a little bit longer.

Ralph Waldo Emerson wrote, "My chief want in life is someone who shall make me do what I can." As you read this chapter, commit to a project of finding someone who will mentor you and help you see more, who will help you do what you can more fully.

2. Mentors Can Give You Productivity and Workplace Performance Ideas

One of the reasons people give us for *not* starting the project that is stuck is that they don't have enough—you guessed it—time. But is it really a matter of time? Sometimes another perspective may be needed to enhance productivity and performance, and you may greatly benefit from informal mentoring and just-in-time coaching.

As an executive workflow coach for more than 15 years, Jason knows this is where he can really help his clients. To start a year-long coaching relationship, he goes to the client's office and spends two full days observing and assessing his client's practices. That way, Jason is able to identify the compromised systems and broken processes he sees as an outside observer that his client cannot see because he or she is so close to the work.

He teaches his clients to work differently so that they can free up 30–60 minutes every day. If you can meet with someone who can give you ideas on how to be more organized and more productive, you'll be able to get around to working on that project that's stuck!

3. Mentors Help You Find Smart People

There's a saying—"If you're the smartest person in the room, then you're in the wrong room." Have you ever felt like you were the smartest person in the room? When that happens, we encourage you to do one of two things: (1) Invite smarter people in or (2) leave to find people smarter than you! Mentors can introduce you to smart people and others whom you wouldn't have access to otherwise.

In 2013, we hosted our first Get Momentum Leadership Retreat in Ojai, California. During one of the afternoon mastermind sessions, an attendee shared a story of building her "team of influencers." She told the group that she had been spending less time with a couple of the people on her original list. When asked why, she replied: "If they're not who I want to be like, why would I continue spending time with them?"

We host these Retreats so that Get Momentum members (and we!) can continually walk into rooms where there are really, really smart people willing to listen, share, and learn together. When seeking a new mentor, we find it's often just as (or more) important to have shared values than a shared industry background.

Creating Your Team

Clearly defining your motivation—your "why"—can get you going. Create a small group of powerful mentors to support you and keep you going when you might feel like quitting. Imagine your work and your life one year from today if you meet regularly—think every month or so—with someone willing to advise you and act as a "sounding board" while you share the ideas you have about what you'd like to get momentum on.

Ask someone you know who has experienced success how they learned to do what they do. Often they will tell you about their mentors. If you're lucky, they'll share stories of the sacrifices they made, the payoff of persistence and their lucky breaks.

Do yourself a favor: identify at least three people you can learn from as you get momentum on your project. Would you like to get more done, faster? Expand your circle of influencers to include experienced mentors willing to share their time and experience with you.

Jodi's Momentum Experience

It can be tough to access some people with experience that would be helpful for me to know about. I know that attending conferences is where and when I can connect with people with similar interests in a casual and conversational environment.

I enjoy attending conferences that are not industry specific, like The Do Lectures. These events attract a wide variety of people from many backgrounds, and I get to meet people outside my immediate social circles.

I also enjoy organizing my own events, everything from going to dinner parties to joining book clubs to hosting morning #CoffeeChat discussion groups. These kinds of gatherings are great ways to be the hub of a group and meet new, potential mentors. By hosting and attending these kinds of events, I've gained a reputation in the community as someone who is always building and growing, and that makes it even easier to connect with people.

GET MOMENTUM ACTIVITY #8: Whom Can I Learn From?

Open your Momentum Journal. Answer the Stage 2 Momentum Question again: "Whom can I learn from?"
Then...

1. Make a list of at least three people you've learned the *most* from (about life, about work, about love, about your profession) and who you think has experience in working on projects like the one you want to start.

(*continued*)

(continued)

2. Reflect again on your answer to the Stage 1 Momentum Question: "What do I want to be known for?" Now, identify one of the people on your list you think could ask you a new question or give you another idea that could help you start the project that's stuck.

3. E-mail, write, or call that person and ask if they'll sit down with you for an hour or so sometime in the next month to discuss your project.

Others' Responses

Here's what two Get Momentum members shared recently:

"Until I expanded my definition of what a mentor is, I didn't think I had many. I realize that by focusing on someone else's success to learn from them, I can get momentum on more goals faster than ever before. Now I know I can be mentored by quite a few people I already know!"

And,

"Earlier in my career, I was told that mentoring was a formal process. I'd even been assigned mentors at school and at work, and it didn't work. After asking, "Whom do I know I can learn from?" I began to meet with and learn from people in more informal ways. Doing so, I felt the freedom to ask better, more meaningful questions. This makes all the difference.

There's no doubt in our minds that when you clarify and commit to a meaningful reason for starting the project that's stuck, meeting with mentors will help you in ways you can only begin to imagine right now. But you do need to find your own mentors."

Being "assigned" a mentor isn't the kind of relationship we're talking about.

Just Knowing It's Possible

We all need someone to look up to, someone we can call our coach, teacher, or mentor. Once you clarify your motives for action (Stage 1), look for someone who's a little farther along the path than you are. Whether this person is someone you know and can call to meet once a month for coffee, or someone you'll have to learn from via their books, e-mail newsletters, or social media feeds, you can set yourself up to learn a lot from their examples.

Once you know what you want to be known for, start looking for examples of who is already known in that regard. Knowing that someone is successful at what you want to do is enough to get you started.

We have found that people you might never meet also have much to teach you. You never even have to meet a mentor; simply learning about someone's success and their journey could be enough to make what you want to happen, happen.

Here's an example:

Professional running in the 1940s and 1950s was dominated by a handful of people worldwide. In 1954, professional runners, coaches and spectators gathered together at Iffley Road Track in Oxford, England. Several runners came together to achieve the previously unachieved—and coveted—"four-minute-mile." Running a mile in four minutes translates to a speed of 15 miles per hour.

On the evening of May 6, 1954, a medical student named Roger Bannister indeed did run a four-minute mile, something that had not been achieved in the history of running. Subsequently, that record has been met time and time again.

How is that possible? How has something deemed unattainable before 1954 become commonplace? (There have been several high school runners who've run sub four-minute miles!)

As soon as athletes saw Roger Bannister achieve that goal, they believed it was possible. And once other runners believed it, they aspired to achieve it.

So, think about it again: Whom could you follow, meet, and/or talk with who can help you see what's possible? Seek them out, meet with them, and share what you're working on. When you meet a mentor who appreciates the purpose statement you've designed—"What you want to be known for"—you'll be in a position of power, learning more, faster, easier than ever before.

Like Attracts Like; Success Attracts Success

Get out from behind your desk. Stop hiding behind e-mail or social media posts. And leave your house or office! If you're going to make progress on your project, you must spend more time with different people. Sure, your current network has been supportive of you getting to this point, but research shows they may *not* be the ones to get you where you want to go!

Martial arts expert Bruce Lee said, "Adapt what is useful, reject what is useless and add what is specifically your own."

Get Momentum Member Experience

One of our Get Momentum members, Victoria, is a photographer. When it was time to go to the next level professionally, we came up with an interesting plan. We suggested that she make a list of 30 galleries within a 30-mile radius of her home. Over a three-month period, she attended the gallery openings, subscribed to their newsletter lists, and even connected with some of the owners via social media.

When it came time to "launch" her own show, she started by reaching out to the artists who had shown their work at those galleries. She then shared a few e-mails, was able to schedule some phone calls, and even met a couple of them for an informal #CoffeeChat discussion.

Victoria said what she learned from them helped her prepare for her art shows for the next year as well as avoid some of the expensive mistakes they had made!

> **GET MOMENTUM ACTIVITY #9: Whom Have You Learned from and How Can You Apply It Today?**
>
> Open your Momentum Journal, and spend 15–20 minutes thinking about someone who has mentored you in the past. What was it about that experience that you remember today? How can you draw upon what you learned from them to get started on an important goal?

Collaboration Is Key

Throughout high school, you were directed to do things on your own. You took exams on your own. You prepared research papers largely by yourself. You had to show your own work. Any time you were assigned "group projects," one of two things happened: (1) One person did all the work or (2) everyone did their own work, then mashed it together to turn in.

Then, you arrived in graduate school, took your first job, or started working to achieve a big life or career goal. Suddenly, you had to collaborate more effectively. And how did you learn to do that? How did you go from "individual contributor" to finding someone to model the new behavior you were looking to learn?

Most likely, you found a formal *or* informal mentor. You met someone who would give you advice, and you observed how they were and what they did. With their words and actions, they gave you ideas about how to get to your next level.

GET MOMENTUM ACTIVITY #10: Contacting a Mentor Whom You Know

In your Momentum Journal, make a list of at least five people you consider your mentors. This month, reach out to schedule time with them.

- Invite one of them to meet you for coffee in the morning, or lunch one afternoon.
- Ask one of them to take a walk with you.

Think about the people you know whom you could meet who model what you need to do. Every day, your energy and productivity can be positively or negatively impacted by the people you spend the most time with. Find (and spend time with) the people who can show you how you need to be and what you need to do in order to achieve your goals.

Do you really want to make that change, to achieve that goal? If your heart and mind are both set on getting momentum, we suggest you create an inventory of mentors you can look to as teachers, coaches, and guides.

Remember the example of Roger Bannister running that four-minute mile? Once the world knew it could be done, it was easier to do it again!

GET MOMENTUM ACTIVITY #11: Whom Do You Network With?

Open your calendar and review the next 30 days. No doubt you're already busy and you're scheduled to deliver on several projects. Review your calendar and schedule time to build your professional network.

Find one person—a mentor—who will meet with you once per week for the next month. Set up the agenda ahead of time so that they know you'd like to focus on your career advancement and/or professional growth. These conversations can be as short as a 15-minute coffee break with a colleague at work or an hour video chat with someone in another part of the world.

Meet with different people with different strengths. Your goal is to make a habit of seeking out people to learn from.

Consider the impact this habit could have over the course of a year. If you meet with 12 people over the course of a year, how many more opportunities to grow, connect, and advance would you have? Start now. The busiest people you know might need a month or more to find open time on their calendar. Start now because by then, you'll have practiced some of these meetings and you'll be prepared when your time with them finally rolls around.

The most productive leaders know that to develop a culture of improvement, they need to manage their time in a way that allows for relationship and team building. Make a list of at least four mentors you can meet with in the next four weeks, one each week. Then contact these mentors and schedule face-to-face meetings.

Going Further, Getting Momentum

Going even further, we've expanded our vision of mentors to include people we may never meet, but who can still influence us. They may have celebrity status in the business world or they may no longer be alive. These kinds of people continue to inspire, motivate, and guide us. We also include organizations, conferences, and companies in the mix. We want good ideas and uplifting stories.

The TED videos (see the website www.TED.com) showcase experts and speakers with "Ideas Worth Sharing." They are great examples of how complete strangers can immediately and forever impact the way we think and even act.

GET MOMENTUM ACTIVITY #12: Meeting a Mentor Whom You Don't Know

Most successful people want to help. Do the prep and background work so they know you're serious. Be genuine. Then ask. (If you don't ask, the answer is "no.") Propose your idea so they know how much of a commitment you're asking for. Be prepared for them to give you a task to do before they agree. Yes, this is a test to see how serious, persistent, and capable you are.

It's important to start by researching their experience. If there is a biography written about them, then read it. If there is an "About" page on their website, then print it and study it. If there is a news article about their work or if they have a YouTube channel dedicated to their work, then learn as much as you can.

Put their advice to work, and keep journal entries of your experiences using their recommendations. Send them updates of your progress: the successes, completions, and challenges that you're still working on. They may or may not reply to give you feedback, based on your agreement. It's your job as the mentee to communicate, follow up, and track agreements. They'll let you know if you need to send fewer updates.

You might consider giving something to them before you make "an ask." Over time, Jason has left comments on articles people have written online, shared their social media updates with his communities, and written reviews on their books or other products on websites.

When you do reach out to these people, let them know very specifically what it is you're looking to do or improve on.

In your note, phone call, or meeting, you're looking to share with them the one thing you're working on that you know they could help you learn about.

Let them know what you've already implemented that is based (even loosely) on what you've learned from them. Then, share your project and what you believe they could help you think through. While they are talking, listen carefully, take notes, and end the conversation by deciding the one strategy you're going to implement based on their ideas.

Lighten Your Load

In the simplest of senses, modeling is "learning by observing someone's behavior." What we think we can (or can't) do is often reinforced when we watch someone else do (or not do) it.

It takes a confident person to step up and ask for input and guidance. How many people do you know who eagerly raise their hand publicly to say, "I don't know how to do what I've been asked to do. Will you help me learn how by modeling what you've done so I can keep going? Oh, and by the way, I'll ultimately do it a little bit differently than you—I hope that's okay."

Starting, especially when you're stuck, is hard enough. Make things just a little bit easier—and lighten your load—by spending time with someone willing to share their journey with you.

GET MOMENTUM ACTIVITY #13: Learning from a Mentor You Don't Know

Who comes to mind as a role model whom you don't know, haven't met, and might not ever meet? Steve Jobs? Oprah? You get the point. It might be a "thought leader" in your

(continued)

(*continued*)

professional field or a celebrity whom you've looked up to over the years.

Just because you don't know this person doesn't mean you can't learn from him or her. You can learn from these people by doing homework and being observant. You can learn from mentors you don't know in at least four ways:

1. Follow them on social media. Along the way, you'll see what they do to expand their business or grow personally and professionally.
2. Retweet something they write, leave a comment on an article they wrote, share one of their updates with your community—these are all methods to engage with these people in ways that could bring you closer to them.
3. Consume the content they create: articles, blog posts, podcasts.
4. Attend a presentation or workshop they present.

Jason's Momentum Experience

More than 20 years ago, I realized I had a lot to learn from people who have books written about them. One day I was at a local bookstore, and I found six books about Benjamin Franklin. I found two books in the biography section written by professional historians, teachers at universities who had often spent a great portion of their careers lecturing on that one person's life they wrote about. Four of the books were on the shelves in the young adult/children's section.

Over the next month, I read them all. I also watched biographies on the History Channel and A&E and found a few more references in encyclopedias in the library of the high school I was teaching at. I still quote some of what I learned from Mr. Franklin. Learning about him changed the way I think, plan, and even get things done. I believe I'm more productive because of what I read two decades ago.

Several times a year I pick a historical leader and spend 10 to 30 hours that month learning about the person as well as his or her life and accomplishments. My intention is to spend at least 30 minutes a day reading, watching, or listening to learn about their life. I've learned so much that I use today from these people.

Record What You Learn

Keep track of your growth as you experiment using what you learn from your mentors. Go to your Momentum Journal once a week (or more) to capture your journey. Make lists of what you've done and of course what you learned. Over the course of a month or two, you'll be able to track and assess your mentors' influences on what you do and how you're getting it done.

Finally, find out whom *they* are learning from. More and more, people are going on the record sharing who their mentors are. As you learn more about them and their path of getting from where they were to where they are, you may discover who helped them along the way.

Subsequently, you may get even more ideas on how you can get your project unstuck and completed.

To Do and Share

1. Create a list of people who could be your mentors. List people you know, as well as a few you haven't met—yet—whom you can still learn from.
2. Carefully choose a few people to discuss that project you're starting or that change you're making. If you see

(continued)

(*continued*)

them get excited for you, or start to share ideas with you, consider choosing them as a mentor.

3. Invite one to three possible mentors to meet with you sometime in the next month. Prepare to discuss a specific milestone (read on to the next chapter!) with them.

Coming Up Next

In the next chapter, we work on taking some of those big, hairy, audacious goals of yours and identifying manageable milestones to help alleviate the pressure and feeling overwhelm.

FIVE STAGES OF MOMENTUM

Stage 1—Motivation
What do I want to be known for?

Stage 2—Mentors
Whom can I learn from?

Stage 3—Milestones
What are three subprojects I can complete?

Stage 4—Monitor
What positive things are happening that I can acknowledge?

Stage 5—Modify
What one change can I make to keep moving forward?

5

Milestones

The safest road to hell is the gradual one—the gentle slope, soft underfoot, without sudden turnings, without milestones, without signposts.

—C. S. Lewis

There's really no honor in proving that you can carry the entire load on your own shoulders. And...it's lonely."

—Amanda Palmer

No matter how great the talent or efforts, some things just take time. You can't produce a baby in one month by getting nine women pregnant.

—Warren Buffett

WHAT ARE THREE SUBPROJECTS I CAN COMPLETE?

What Are Milestones, Really?

We define milestones as "significant events in the progress or development of a project that you want to get momentum on."

It's easier to get and keep momentum when you create a schedule for your large, long-term project. When you lay out the work you need to do and organize your activity (and deadlines) three months at a time, in one-month intervals, even the largest projects feel more doable.

Creating subprojects—what we call milestones—removes the burden of trying to get everything done at once, or putting things off until later when you think you'll have more time. Work this way and you won't burn out. In fact, you'll feel the satisfaction of completion along the way, which fuels a feeling of momentum.

Knowing What's Coming

Years ago, we moved to Alaska for the month of August. We drove from Anchorage to Homer on the Kenai Peninsula via beautiful Highway 1. A local client had loaned us their truck and given us a book titled *The Milepost*. It is a travel guide to the Alaskan highways with mile-by-mile details of road conditions, sights, and services.

Jodi affectionately referred to it as "100 Ways to Die in Alaska." Mile by mile, the book described the local hazards of grizzly bear zones (aka "wildlife viewing"), quicksand beaches, and avalanche danger areas. (We're not making this up!)

Jodi *loved* this book. She read ahead while Jason drove. As frightening and foreign as some of those hazards were, it was a relief to know about them in order to avoid them and continue along the Sterling Highway.

Knowing what's coming can be a huge relief when you find yourself struggling with a large, long-term project. Unlike *The Milepost*, you don't have to know every single detail from point A to point B. But in terms of your big project, planning and completing the first three months of subprojects will help you build *and keep* the momentum you need to follow through to the end.

The Power of Milestones

Dividing your large project into smaller subprojects—milestones—is an effective way to get and keep momentum. To create these subprojects, organize your workload in "about" 90-day cycles, planning *achievable* and *believable* outcomes to complete every month or so. Our recommendation is that for every significant project you're working on that you identify a minimum of three specific milestones.

Achievable

Over the years, we've asked members, clients and even friends and family members to tell us about the projects that are stuck. As they explain why they haven't done what they had hoped to do by now—always for a variety of good reasons—we ask them to think about the smaller parts of the project they *could* be working on. We know it's easier this way.

In most cases, people get stuck trying to complete the entire project instead of working on subprojects that—when completed—could get them closer to the finish line.

Sure, thinking big is important. But—and this is a big *but*—you've got to divide those big goals into *achievable* subprojects.

Believable

Napoleon Hill wrote several books, and one of Jason's favorites is called *Think and Grow Rich*, which was published in 1937. That's right, he wrote this book during the Great Depression in the United States! Hill wrote: "Whatever the mind of man can conceive and believe, it can achieve."

As you identify milestones to complete, be sure that they are *believable*. For each milestone you commit to, ask, "Do I believe it's possible to do that?" To make a subproject seem more believable, make it a little bit smaller. What we know is this: An action identified and then completed—no matter how big or small—will create momentum you will use to take another next step. Little by little, you'll make progress. And that is the goal.

GET MOMENTUM ACTIVITY #14: Three Subprojects I Can Complete

Go to your Momentum Journal, and after setting a timer for 30 minutes, write a list of things you think of when you think about your project.

This shouldn't be a to-do list, a timeline, or a plan. Simply write anything you can think of related to that project—big things, little things, short term, and long term.

Start by listing the names of people you think of when you think of that project as well as any "like-products or like-projects" you can think of related to your project. Aim for at least 50 line items; 100 is even better.

If you find not much happened during those 30 minutes, one of two things occurred:

1. Your project isn't really that big, meaning it probably won't take a whole 90 days to complete. And that's fine. We simply want to give you the opportunity to take on a big project, the one that you've been hoping you could get to for a long time now. So, you have some options: Keep on working on this one as you finish the book *Get Momentum*. Or go back to Stage 1 and review your answers to identify an even bigger project you want to take on.

2. You thought too much. Your frontal cortex got in the way as you started judging what you wrote and that prevented you from remembering all the things that you've been thinking of recently. If this happened, start

again—right now. Make a promise to yourself that you will brainstorm a list of 50 things about your project. Trust us, you can do it.

Review your list and determine the next three "milestones." These should be intervals—subprojects—that are spaced around 30 days apart. When completed, each subproject will serve as a major boost to your overall progress. See the following example of subprojects for a large project we plan every year.

Examples of Planning the Get Momentum Leadership Retreat

Annually, we host the Get Momentum Leadership Retreat in Ojai, California. We know it's easier to plan a successful retreat when we think in terms of 30-, 60-, and 90-day blocks of time. Here's how we used milestones to meet a September deadline for our Retreat.

Milestone	Subproject	Due Date
1	Finalize all marketing materials and implement the enrollment plan on the website	July 1
2	Finalize curriculum for the three-day retreat	August 1
3	Finalize logistics (attendees, catering, travel, etc.)	September 1

These milestones help us stay focused on the priorities according to the timeline they need to be handled within. The 30-day time frame gives us the freedom to focus on what's next and not get overwhelmed by all the pieces of the project at one time.

Setting milestones is a freeing experience and one that takes practice in assessing how long it takes you to do things.

Of course, every year that we plan one of these events, new ideas get added at the project and task levels. The clearer we are about the motivation for hosting the retreats, the easier it is to know what the subprojects need to be.

Be aware: No one milestone by itself is enough to complete the project. In fact, in isolation, each one of those subprojects could actually cause more frustration than momentum. Imagine if we'd finalized the Retreat's curriculum, but never made time to focus on marketing the program!

Why Three Subprojects?

The magic of three subprojects is based on our experience of just how far you can look out and plan achievable and believable subprojects. If you space out the next three milestones of your project about a month apart, you'll experience the iterative process of completing work along the way.

Of course, you can have a year-long strategy, as most businesses and even families have, but you'll still want to work in terms of three subprojects spread out every 90 days or so. Make sure you review and update your overall goals and objectives (at work and in life) against your long-term goals a few times each year. About monthly, however, we suggest you review the next three months of major milestones and reconcile your progress against those.

The 30/30 Rule

A secret to getting momentum on a project that is stuck is the 30/30 Rule. This strategy is easy to understand, but it can be challenging to implement.

Every day, work for 30 undistracted, uninterrupted, completely intentional minutes on one specific aspect of your project that is not due for 30 days or more from today. The 30-day increments are important here. A month is about enough time to make significant progress. It's long enough to get some real work done. Just think, by adopting the 30/30 Rule, within 30 days you could have worked 15 hours on your project!

When you sit down to write that copy for your website, draft that sketch for your next piece, or brainstorm the workflow for that app you want to publish, turn off everything and everyone else. Set a timer and then get to work on that one thing.

Note that we've found that working more consistently every day for 30-minute sessions is better than putting projects off until "later," and then spending an entire weekend or staying up late to get something done at the last minute. If for just 30 minutes a day you can take action on a part of your project that isn't due for 30 days, imagine what you will accomplish.

Suddenly, it will be a month from now, and... voilà! You'll have fewer emergencies and fewer fires to put out.

GET MOMENTUM ACTIVITY #15: Practice the 30/30 Rule

Start practicing now. Find 30 minutes *today* and spend that block of time working on something that isn't due for 30 days or more. The easiest way to do this is to pick a personal project that is happening one to three months from today. Practice with a personal project, and then apply the idea to your work goals.

Is there a birthday, celebration or blended-trip (work and personal) coming up in the next quarter? Spend 30 minutes thinking about and planning some of the details you know you'll have to handle.

Are there tickets you can put on hold, or reservations you can make?

Are there people you want to connect with while you're there?

Is there a gift you want to purchase ahead of time, thereby saving money *and* making sure that you get it in plenty of time?

(continued)

(*continued*)

Of course, the above questions are all about the "personal" side of things. Create your own checklist of things you'd want to think of ahead of time as you think of professional and community-based goals.

Jason's Momentum Experience

I had a dream of working with clients for five days in a row in the same city. It's actually one of the reasons I left my previous job. My manager didn't believe it was possible. I thought it was… as long as we had the right mindset, strategies, commitment and put a plan into action.

Since 2000, my presentation schedule has been booked three to nine months in advance in cities around the world (www .WhereIsWomack.com). Often, I was scheduled to speak for just a day per city I visit. For example, I would fly on Monday to facilitate a seminar in Chicago on Tuesday; another flight on Wednesday to facilitate a seminar in New York City; then off to London on Saturday for presentations on Monday and Tuesday; and a flight back to California the following Wednesday. This was a normal schedule for me; of course, it was fine when I was in my early 30s. But I always knew that it wasn't a sustainable lifestyle.

Just after founding our own training firm in 2007, I ran an experiment, working for 30 minutes a week e-mailing, following up with, and calling clients to tell them I was working in their city later that quarter. Within a year, I began organizing two, three, or even four days of work in the same city.

This was progress!

Then one day in 2015 I achieved a major milestone: I worked 5 days in a row for one client (the global company has more than 4,000 employees in New York City alone).

Not only did I get to check into one hotel for six nights, I was scheduled to coach clients on the same floor of the company's headquarters in Midtown. Rather than dealing with all kinds of special logistics, I was able to focus 100 percent on serving my clients. It's also a more profitable business model for us as well as more sustainable on my physical body now that I'm in my mid-40s!

It made me rethink my business development strategy. Now, I spend *at least* two 30-minute sessions each week just looking into how to build business opportunities that are 90 days out.

The 90/90 Rule

Okay, if you liked the 30/30 Rule, you're going to love this one. One day per month, spend 90 minutes looking out 90 or more days.

Consider the last time you sat down to work on a project. How did you get that time? Perhaps you blocked it out on your calendar. Or, maybe you had a free afternoon on a weekend, or a meeting at work was cancelled at the last minute.

We recommend at least once each month you *jump ahead* and review your calendar 90 days out and pick something to focus on. The 90/90 Rule is when you spend 90 minutes working on, thinking about and organizing something that isn't due to be completed (or even worked on) for 90 or more days from now.

This 90/90 Rule is an investment. It's the time you need to get out from managing the pressure of the day-to-day and emergencies. Implementing this strategy takes some getting used to, but after a few months of looking forward anticipating what's coming and planning to be prepared, you'll find fewer deadlines sneak up on you.

Get Momentum Member Experience

Felice Martinez of Petaluma, California, told us: "I grew up thinking that I had to have the whole project figured out before I could even begin. When I started my own health and wellness consulting practice, I realized that there was just too much to know and way too much to do. I used the milestone strategy to complete very clear and specific pieces of my long-term projects in 90-day cycles.

The more I completed, the more energy I felt! I've gotten more done than I thought possible."

GET MOMENTUM ACTIVITY #16: Implementing the 90/90 Rule

Review your calendar this month and schedule a 90-minute meeting with yourself. Find a day of the week you are confident that you'll be able to "keep the meeting." (You don't want this one to become "overcome by events." Stick to your plan!)

To prepare, open your Momentum Journal and identify a *big* project you will start working on three to six months from today. Again, it can be work *or* personal, just make sure that you're going to still be working on it 90 days from now.

On the day you'll practice this 90/90 planning session, make sure you have the tools you will need. Among the gear we always recommend:

Your "To-Do List" system. During your thinking time, you're going to come up with actions that you need to do or delegate in the short to mid term. Write them on your to-do list, so they get done sooner than later.

Your e-mail management system. No doubt you're going to come up with *something* you'll need to ask or send someone. Have your e-mail handy, but don't get distracted by the inbox!

Your calendar (professional *and* personal). Surely, you'll come up with some ideas that you need to park on your calendar as a reminder one week, one month, or even one quarter from today.

The purpose of practicing this 90/90 Rule thinking is to feel what it's like—90 or more days from today—to have already started thinking, before you needed to have started thinking!

Create Your Future

Management thinker Peter Drucker once said, "The best way to predict the future is to create it." That's what happens as you implement the 30/30 the 90/90 Rules to work with milestone planning. Three months at a time, you're planning and designing your future.

When reading these strategies, they make sense. In fact, you may be nodding your head in agreement. It's important to know *why* thinking in terms of milestones is so powerful for getting momentum. We want you to understand the purpose of this strategy so that you're more likely to work this way and accomplish things more efficiently and effectively.

When you commit yourself to a smaller piece of a large project, something that is due in just 30 days, you make it easier to reach the finish line, subproject by subproject.

GET MOMENTUM ACTIVITY #17: Working On a Shared Vision

By the way, are you working on something with a partner or a colleague? The more you each know about where you are going, and what it will look like when you get there, the easier it is to choose what to work on for 30 minutes a day and 90 minutes each month. Include these people in your planning so you are on the same page in how to complete your large project.

Thinking in terms of milestones, subprojects, and timed workflow sessions (30/30 and 90/90) puts you in the driver's seat of control of the thing that is stuck. You can improve how you set milestones and how you work smarter to achieve what you set out to accomplish.

For one, we encourage you to focus on the emotion of the outcome. One of the best things you can do is identify an

(continued)

(*continued*)

"Ideal Day" for the future. Jason wrote about this in his book *Your Best Just Got Better: Work Smarter, Think Bigger, Make More*, and has been teaching leaders to think about Ideal Days since he started doing in 1995.

Jason noted, "Once, while complaining about the organization I worked with, my mentor asked me a simple question. Ron said, 'Jason, would you know a good day if you saw one?' In that moment, I realized that I was so used to seeing the problems that, in fact, I wouldn't have noticed a good day!"

A Note of Caution

You may be saying, "But I don't have time to work on projects that are 90 or even 30 days away! I'm already busy working on what's due tomorrow!" Trust us, we know what you're feeling. This wasn't something that we started because it was easy. But, the more we work this way, the more we realize the benefits.

We encourage you to use the 30/30 Rule because it will—within a month to six weeks—pay off. You'll be ahead of the game, up to date and you'll have relieved some of the stress of working on things until the last minute.

Before you know it, you'll be ahead of schedule, less stressed, and more on track to complete the project on time, or even ahead of schedule.

The real work is, well, *doing the work*. However, the fact that you're reading a book called *Get Momentum: How to Start When You're Stuck* means that you want to improve your habits to work most effectively and efficiently.

To Do and Share

1. People burn out when they try to do everything all at once. When you don't get to finish some part of the project, you may become discouraged. Pick one of your big projects and create three mini-project milestones that will help guide you. By dividing the grand plan into smaller, independent, and easy-to-complete subprojects, you'll get your chance to experience a few wins along the way.
2. The 30/30 Rule: Work for 30 minutes on something that is not due for at least 30 days.
3. The 90/90 Rule: Work for 90 minutes once each month on a specific outcome or goal that isn't due for 90 days or more.

Coming Up Next

The more clear you are about the milestones of the project you're working on, the easier it is to know when to ask for help. In the next chapter, you learn about the importance of monitoring progress. When you monitor your workflow and workload using detailed and specific criteria, you're able to identify what's working and what's not. Chapter 6 addresses the powerful impact of acknowledgement, and will also put you in a position to start thinking about the subtle changes to make.

FIVE STAGES OF MOMENTUM

Stage 1—Motivation
What do I want to be known for?

Stage 2—Mentors
Whom can I learn from?

Stage 3—Milestones
What are three subprojects I can complete?

Stage 4—Monitor
What positive things are happening that I can acknowledge?

Stage 5—Modify
What one change can I make to keep moving forward?

6

Monitor

Measure twice; cut once.

—English proverb

What gets measured, gets managed.

—Peter Drucker

If I had an hour to solve a problem, I'd spend 55 minutes thinking about the problem and 5 minutes thinking about solutions.

—Albert Einstein

WHAT POSITIVE THINGS ARE HAPPENING THAT I CAN ACKNOWLEDGE?

What Do You Need to Monitor, Really?

One beautiful spring morning in New York City, Jason and Jodi met with their mentor, Frances Hesselbein, in her third-floor office at the corner of Park Avenue between 50th and 51st Street (www.HesselbeinInstitute.org). During the meeting, she held tightly to one of each of their hands and asked them to look out over the city.

She said, "Look out this window." She paused before continuing, "Tell me what is visible to you that is not yet seen by the people you serve."

Now, you need to know that it was Frances' mentor—the author Peter Drucker—who taught *her* to think about that question while she was CEO of the Girl Scouts of the United States of America from 1976 to 1990. As you learn about Peter's work, you'll find he often said, "I don't predict. I just look out the window and see what's visible but not yet seen."

While working toward your milestones, keep your eyes open. Identify the indicators that you're on course to achieve what you set out to accomplish. And, be on the lookout to realize when you're slipping off course. The sooner you know, the better. Identify specific indicators so that you can check to ensure you're on track and making progress. Create a dashboard so you can review all the indicators you're tracking.

When tracking indicators, we strongly suggest you use quantitative terms—numbers, time, money, distances, total products, clicks, pages written, anything that can you measure.

For example, when Jason trained for his first full-length marathon (Los Angeles, 2016), he built a dashboard to track his progress on three of the important milestones 90 days before the event:

1. Miles per run
2. Running days per week
3. Hours of sleep per night

The more specific you are, the better. Look, maybe you're not training to run a marathon, but you've got something that you want to accomplish. In this chapter, we coach you to monitor your progress, so that you can acknowledge advances and make real-time, real-life modifications along the way. We'll cover making modifications in Chapter 7.

Additionally, we'll tell you how important it is to monitor the progress of other people on your team. Pay attention to what they accomplish, what matters to them, and what's working for them. Notice them for what they do by focusing on the positive results they achieve. Do this regularly and you'll achieve more than you ever thought possible.

Momentum creates more momentum. Read on and you'll see that acknowledging accomplishment—what you get done, and what people around you get done—is a way of working that will create positive momentum.

The Power of Monitoring

When you set up a solid system and a sustainable process to monitor your progress, you make it easier to recognize what's working and when you need to take course-corrective action. Think about it: Figuring out what happened and why it happened is a competitive advantage. When you acknowledge that the work you do creates results, it's easier to build on the wins.

Ben Fanning, author of *The Quit Alternative: The Blueprint for Creating the Job You Love…Without Quitting*, told us: "Conquering burnout doesn't have to start with quitting your job; it starts with recognizing how the work you do matters. Monitoring your progress over time helps you recognize the wins that you might have overlooked otherwise."

Now, if you're asking yourself if it's worth it, if you're wondering whether there's going to be value in setting up processes and systems to be notified when things are going well—and of course when a plan is going off course—just think about this: What would happen if you applied this strategy to the project you want to start?

Once you identify your 30-, 60-, and 90-day milestones, wouldn't you want some kind of a "dashboard-like" system that would show you when you're doing well, and when you need to make small changes early in the process? As you recognize the effort it took to achieve milestones along the way, you acknowledge success and celebrate the wins.

At this point, you're rewarding the part of your brain that needs that acknowledgment. Reward yourself and your team for work done well and you build confidence for everyone who's interested in moving things forward.

Dr. Larry Brilliant gave an excellent TED Talk in 2006. During the presentation, he reiterated a call to action: "Early detection, early response." Considering his life's goal is to eradicate global pandemics, it would make sense that he wants health professionals to be working on systems, processes, and diagnoses that would make the indicators of the spread of disease show up sooner. When you have the information you need, you can take action quickly!

Jason's Momentum Experience

On a Sunday evening, I called Anne-Marie (not her real name), a new Get Momentum member who is a senior manager in a local charity organization. Her program received funding to create and provide a junior high/high school leadership program in the San Francisco Bay Area. Her first project: to create and pilot an after-school leadership development program in partnership with 15 local libraries. The libraries already had after-school homework centers; Anne-Marie thought more could be done than just help students study for tests at school.

During our call, I asked what her goals were for the next year.

"I want the program to make a positive difference and hopefully have a big impact in the community," she said. There was a hint of doubt in her voice as she ended the sentence in a high tone, as if she were asking me.

It was clear that her goals, although well-intentioned, were indefinite, vague, and unmeasurable.

We talked for an hour that evening to clarify specific metrics of what making a "positive difference" would look, sound, and feel like. Of course, we divided her milestones into 30-day segments, with a promise to return and review her progress at the end of 90 days. During subsequent conversations, we reviewed milestones she identified and compared her results to the plans she had.

Over time, she clarified and updated her answers (yes, more than one!) to the first Momentum Question, "What do you want to be known for?" We spent the next year working in 90-day cycles. She committed to milestones that were achievable and believable. She also designed a monitoring dashboard that she used at the end of each week to know how close she was to achieving her goal of "making a difference" based on specific criteria that she had chosen.

GET MOMENTUM ACTIVITY #18: When Do You Fill Up?

You're driving through town when you're momentarily distracted by a flashing light on your dashboard indicating that the gas tank is almost empty. It's not a matter of *if* you'll refuel, but when and where you'll stop to fill the tank.

Open your Momentum Journal to record your responses to the questions below.

1. Do you let the gas tank "almost empty" light remind you to refuel? Does it ever surprise you?
2. Would your response (how much farther you drive or how soon you find a service station) depend on who else is in the car?
3. Would your location impact your decision to get gas a little sooner?

Ask yourself similar questions when you review progress on milestones you've identified.

1. Do you wait until the last minute to prepare for the task you need to work on next? Do these deadlines ever surprise you?
2. Would your response (how much you try to do on your own or how soon you ask for help) depend on who else is working on the project with you?
3. Would the size, scale or importance of the project impact your decision to ask for help a little sooner?

When you define milestones that are one, two, and three months out, you can plan the time and resources it takes to achieve them. And you will be able to tell if you're off course along the way. Build a monitoring system that gives you the information you can use to make better decisions about what to do next, ask for help as soon as you need it, and take course-corrective action appropriately. This will save you time and money in addition to getting more things done, better.

Know the Course to Stay the Course

When we arrived to meet with the CEO and senior staff of a medium-sized tech business in central California, we were immersed in their culture of "monitoring."

On a wall in the lobby, several computer monitors hung at eye level, each one showing multiple data streams—a pulse on significant aspects of the organization. As we walked around, we saw that on many walls, above each copy machine, and in the conference room, monitors tracked data! We were told that the data refreshed every 15 minutes.

This company is serious about monitoring its key indicators in real time. Within moments of an indicator flashing red, the appropriate teams are notified. But more than that, since the installation of these public displays, employees are encouraged to raise their hands when they see (or intuit) that something is *about* to go off course.

Now, does your productivity system need to be set up so you would know if you're on or off course by glancing at a wall (or a screen or a notebook)? It depends. What are you trying to accomplish?

Monitor What Matters (to Make Change More Quickly)

Here's a question for you: As you're driving to a restaurant you've never been to before to meet someone who is very, very important to you, how soon would you want to know that you're off course?

Without regularly monitoring your progress, you might drift off course without noticing. We've all trusted a GPS system more than we should. You've probably had that gut feeling that the restaurant is not in the direction the GPS is directing you. But you go in that direction anyway because the GPS is instructing you that way. Next thing you know, you've missed your reservation or you're lost or both!

Surely, you would want to know you're off course right away so you could recalculate and get back on track.

We encourage you to create indicators that you monitor so you get good data to make decisions.

GET MOMENTUM ACTIVITY #19: I'll Know I'm Off Course If...

Open your Momentum Journal and answer these questions:

1. What specific indicators would tell you if you're on or off course for achieving your milestone?
2. What are five criteria that you can monitor?
   (Think quantitative: What can you count, measure, or track? Numbers, time, dollar amounts, etc.)

Jodi's Momentum Experience

When I took over our personal and company finances from Jason, I assumed that would be a huge stress relief for him. What I didn't realize was that he still had our finances on his mind because I wasn't telling him what I was monitoring and the decisions I was making. What I thought would relieve his stress by not "bothering" him with any of the details, actually added to his worries!

After we talked about monitoring our finances—the personal and company numbers—I created the "Money Monday" report. I email him a high-level summary of the company's cash flow. The indicators I track include the overview of the company's income, accounts receivables, expenses, and anticipated quarterly projections. This information is enough to let him relax and trust that our finances are being managed well. Knowing where we are financially allows us to forecast and make informed decisions.

Stress can come from a misunderstanding of how much information someone wants to receive. What does your team, boss, or partner really need to know to feel like he or she is in the loop but not bogged down with all the details?

Do you have a big-stress situation stemming from miscommunication? Set up your own status report and ask your team members what kind of information they need in order to relax and trust that you're handling the situation so they can really let go.

Emergence versus Emergency

The intersection of these two words is really interesting to Jason. How do we identify an emerging milestone and be sure it does not become an emergency? The goal is to go from "Here's an idea" to "Hey, look, I'm ahead of schedule. I'm on track. I'm making progress, and I'm getting things done."

Regular monitoring of your milestones and progress ensures that emerging things don't become emergencies.

Hindsight Really Is 20/20—So Take Advantage of It

Few people take advantage of their "20/20 wisdom" as a regular part of their business cycle. How often do you take the time to do a thorough debriefing of a work project? Fewer people we know still apply any kind of a review process to their personal goals and dreams. We have cycles to work and life, and if you pause to reflect on the progress you've made and how far you have to go, you'll put yourself in a position to be both strategic and tactical in your approach to getting things done.

Think about the last project you finished. If you don't stop and document what you learned, the insights you gained—and what you'd do differently—those details will disappear from your memory. Research shows details are forgotten about four to six days after completing the task. Unfortunately, many people don't do a debriefing session with their team or their family because they're already busy planning the next project or event.

The purpose of a project debrief is to find better ways of doing things. You can do this by identifying mistakes that were made and resources that were wasted. By clarifying the lessons learned, you'll save time and money the next time you work on a similar project.

GET MOMENTUM ACTIVITY #20:
The Debriefing Process

Take some time after your next event or project to think about what you would or would not do again. Two important outcomes of the debriefing process are:

1. To learn from and repeat what worked
2. To share and teach best practices for future success

Go to your Momentum Journal and answer the following questions. Answer them on your own, then sit down with a mentor, colleague, or family member to discuss.

1. **What worked especially well?** What parts would you want to repeat if or when you do this again? What factors worked in your favor?
2. **What aspects did not work?** Did you miss something entirely? What assumptions did you make that backfired? What areas needed more support than you expected? What took more time than you budgeted for? What lessons did you learn? Where was there confusion?
3. **What were the biggest risks you took?** Did they turn out as you expected? Were they worth it? Did you take enough risks? What surprised you? How well did you handle those surprises? How could you better prepare for a surprise factor?
4. **If money, time, and resources were not a factor, what would you do differently next time?** What features, benefits, or goodies would you add? Describe in vivid detail this ideal scene in terms of wild success and flawless execution.

Stop the Cycle of Repeating Mistakes

Don't buy into crisis management. Most crises can be anticipated and avoided with the right planning and attention. If you're shaking your head and saying, "No, I'm always in crisis mode," then you need to implement the debriefing process immediately and build it into your culture! You don't have the luxury of not requiring this essential aspect of project management.

By making the debriefing session part of your routine, you add an effective planning tool to your management skill set and to your organization's future. Monitor your next few subprojects or events for lessons learned, and build a legacy of continual improvement. Include your team in the debrief process so they learn from the wisdom of 20/20 hindsight.

Appreciation Is Key

Employees thrive in an environment where they feel appreciated. Richard Branson sums it up perfectly: "The way you treat your employees is the way *they* will treat your customers." Be aware of what you're modeling for your team, your family, and your community.

Knowing this, it's up to you to look around and find an opportunity to acknowledge those who deserve it. Showing appreciation is easier than you may think.

However, you have to know what you're looking for. At the start of a day, take time to review your calendar, looking out for the next 24 hours. Ask yourself, "Who out there stands a chance of making my life a little easier?" You see, once you identify someone, you make it easier to find something to acknowledge him or her for.

At the end of the day, pause for some reflection. Did something happen *near* what you were hoping for? Often, clients ask us whether timing is important. Something powerful happens when you appreciate someone in the moment. However, don't let timing stop you. Make it a practice at the end of the day to engage in some kind of acknowledgment process. You may not always be able to thank the people in person, but writing your acknowledgment about their contribution will create a valuable emotional experience for you. Most people think the value of writing thank you cards is all about the person receiving the card. We think that's only half of the value. The other half is you feeling grateful and appreciative on a daily basis.

Jason's Momentum Experience

Early in my teaching career, I noticed that the only parents who were contacted by the school were those whose child had misbehaved. I wanted to change that model, so I tried an experiment for a week. I stayed after school every day to call my students and their parents at home. I reached out to one student from each of my five classes, for a total of five quick calls each evening.

During each phone call, I shared one positive aspect about the student. I made sure that what I was sharing with these young people was exactly the behavior that I wanted to see again. I *only* told students what they did *right* that day. Maybe they helped a fellow student or they raised their hand to participate in class discussion. Or perhaps they turned in their homework on time. I also told the student's parents how proud I was to be their child's teacher.

An interesting pattern began to develop: The more I acknowledged my students, the more they repeated the acknowledged behavior. And, here's where it got crazy-awesome.

The students started talking among themselves, and pretty soon, they were sharing with each other what I had called about. And other students started acting in ways to receive acknowledgment and get that phone call. And, you know what? Over time, students were acting in ways I had hoped. Some teachers have a discipline plan, I had a *acknowledgment plan*.

I called students and their parents every day for my remaining four years as a teacher.

GET MOMENTUM ACTIVITY #21: What Positive Things Are Happening That I Can Acknowledge?

Take a moment to review your calendar for the next three months. Then, open your Momentum Journal and list five things that you could monitor.

We recommend you monitor these five things in cycles of 30 to 90 days at a time. If you attempt to monitor too much information at once, you'll become overwhelmed by the time it takes to collect, process, and organize all the data. If that happens, you might stop tracking altogether. By selecting five things to watch for, you will:

- Make it easier to observe exactly what's happening.
- Figure out if and when you need to correct your course sooner.
- Notice patterns and processes that you can turn into best practices.

What Does Gratitude Have to Do with It?

So, what was behind Jason's students' good behavior? Believe it or not, gratitude. According to work by postdoctoral researcher Glenn Fox, when the brain feels gratitude, it activates areas responsible for feelings of reward, fairness, and self-reference.

Antonio Damasio, a professor of neuroscience at the University of Southern California, has found that emotions play a central role in social cognition and decision making. He noted, "Gratitude rewards generosity and maintains the cycle of healthy social behavior."

That is to say, whenever you receive an expression of gratitude from someone you trust and who you think is genuine, then you automatically start planning to do whatever you did for them again. So, expressing gratitude to someone results in him or her acting in a way that will elicit more gratitude from you.

We were formally introduced to this "reward" theory when we studied psychology in graduate school. We then put it into everyday practice when we adopted our Black Labrador, Zuma. From our experiences in using gratitude and rewards to get desired behavior, we gleaned two important lessons:

1. Agree on as few rules as possible, but stick to the rules—don't ever break the rule that you make. Ever.
2. Timing is key. Give a positive reward as close to the desired behavior as possible.

Eventually, this process of positive acknowledgment, reward, and behavior became a part of our lives. It easily slipped into our work, our personal relationships, and even our own personal goal setting.

GET MOMENTUM ACTIVITY #22: The End-of-the-Day Process

The best way to acknowledge someone or something positive is to increase your awareness. And you can fine-tune your awareness during the day.

For years, we've personally been doing the following practice as well as teaching it in workshops and in our Get Momentum Leadership Academy, with great results.

At the end of the day, use your Momentum Journal to list the following:

1. **One thing you completed that day.** It's typical to review all the things that didn't get done. Instead, try focusing on something that you finished.
2. **One person you can acknowledge for his or her contribution.** Identify a task that someone did. Recognize the contribution the person made privately, and if appropriate, publicly.
3. **One event or circumstance you are grateful to have heard of or been part of.** Pause long enough to reflect on what went well—specifically, what went in your favor. Again, this practice is for your experience. Sharing your gratitude with them is extra. Maybe someone helped you through a difficult situation. Perhaps you're simply thankful for a friend, a family member, or a colleague at work. The most interesting thing about this strategy is you don't even have to tell them! There is no shortage of what to be grateful for.

Notice When Things Are Working

As you think about the great managers you've worked for, the people you get along with the most, and your relationships with your partner, parents, and children, you'll want to monitor what you're doing and how they're responding.

The more you notice when things are working, the more you'll notice good happening all around you. No, you're not going to turn into one of those "positive thinking" types. Instead, you'll be known as the leader who reflects. The manager who debriefs. The parent who notices. The community member who acknowledges. And, the more you do all of that, the more momentum you will feel.

Momentum Member Experience

During a workshop, Cheryl (not her real name) shared a story with us. She's a portfolio manager in Portland, Oregon, and after learning about the psychology of acknowledging accomplishment, she experimented with it. She said, "I wanted to try this before implementing it with my team here in the office. One morning I mailed an anonymous thank you card to my hairdresser. I didn't put my return address on the envelope or sign my name on the card. I just wrote two paragraphs to let her and her staff know how much I appreciated them and how special I feel when I'm in her salon."

"The following month, I went in for an appointment. I was actually surprised when I noticed the card taped to the wall at the front desk. I'd forgotten I had sent it! Here's the crazy thing: I could read it from my side of the counter. And so could every other customer and all the employees. That was when I realized the power of saying 'thank you.' It goes beyond the five-minute action of writing a note while I'm sitting at my desk."

As she paid for her service that day, Cheryl said, she did not tell her hairdresser that she was the one who wrote the card; it wasn't necessary.

We would not encourage you to write a heartfelt gratitude note with an intention of being recognized for the effort. We discourage you from putting a business card in an acknowledgment card. This is not a marketing tactic; it's a *gratitude plan*. It's not about them getting the card; it's about who you become and how you feel as you write the card!

To Do and Share

1. Build a dashboard of three to five indicators to monitor your progress. This will keep you on course and serve as an early warning system to make changes.
2. Hold a debriefing session after you achieve a milestone. Learn from what went well and what needs to be improved.
3. Build your *gratitude plan* to encourage the behaviors you want from people and to feel the affects of the positive emotions.

Coming Up Next

As you monitor your progress, it's going to be natural to want to make changes. In the next chapter, you'll focus on making small changes based on objective data that you've been monitoring.

FIVE STAGES OF MOMENTUM

Stage 1—Motivation
What do I want to be known for?

Stage 2—Mentors
Whom can I learn from?

Stage 3—Milestones
What are three subprojects I can complete?

Stage 4—Monitor
What positive things are happening that I can acknowledge?

Stage 5—Modify
What one change can I make to keep moving forward?

7

Modify

To really boost your sense of self-efficacy, think of ways you could modify your usual tasks to suit your personal style.

—Martha Beck

If you only do what you can do, you will never be more than you are now.

—Master Po Ping, *Kung Fu Panda 3*

If you set out to do something and you give it your all and it doesn't work out, be willing to modify your goal slightly. Have the ability to look in another direction. A small shift could guide you to the real purposes of your life.

—Halle Berry

WHAT ONE CHANGE CAN I MAKE TO KEEP MOVING FORWARD?

What Does Modify Mean, Really?

"If you're stuck, you're stressed." It was fitting that we saw that on a bumper sticker while driving through stop-and-go traffic in Silicon Valley on our way to a #CoffeeChat at a favorite coffee shop in Menlo Park, CA. Ironically, we were going to meet three new members of the Get Momentum Academy, and with two miles to go, we were stuck in—according to the app on our phone—22 minutes of traffic!

Just a few minutes earlier, we were driving the speed limit and talking about the exciting project that we had just started… writing this book! Suddenly, the brake lights in front of us lit up, the traffic stopped and seconds turned into minutes. The stress grew as well. We're used to momentum, not being stuck in traffic! So, when we saw the bumper sticker, we looked at each other and laughed aloud. It was a beautiful California day, we had plenty of time until our meeting, and we could return to a great conversation. One little change in focus, and we were less stressed.

Just like that.

The dictionary definition of the word *modify* is "to make partial or minor changes that improve the way things are." The fifth stage of momentum is where we start to make small changes.

What if you could gain momentum by making a partial or minor change? Reading this chapter, you'll learn how to start small and make big things happen. You'll use the energy of acknowledging accomplishment you read about in the previous chapter and focus on making specific, targeted changes to your work and your life.

Remember, monitor your actions, notice your wins, and make progress on your milestones. When you do all that, you will feel more successful. The more momentum you feel, the easier it will be to do things differently when the time comes.

That time is *now*.

The Power of Modifying

The more closely you monitor the progress you make on the milestones you set, the sooner you'll know when you're on target to achieve a goal or about to drift off course. And, the more up to date and finely tuned your monitoring system is, the easier it will be to make small changes in real time.

The most important thing to remember when modifying is to *start by noticing what you're doing that isn't getting positive results*. Reflect on what you read in Chapter 1 of this book. "Good" is the enemy of "great." And "good enough" is tempting to maintain.

In this chapter, we'll suggest you make a specific change based on what you're hoping to achieve. Notice, we didn't say changes, we really do mean just *one change at a time*. Too often we see people get motivated, start an important project and then lose momentum within months…sometimes even weeks. Why? They tried to change too much, too fast.

When Should You Modify?

You modify your strategy when you're not achieving your goals. You modify your tactics when the way you're working isn't achieving the results you want. You modify, making small changes when you're not meeting your milestones, when you're feeling stuck, or when it's obvious something is not working.

Are you wondering if you need to be doing things a little bit differently? If so, take some time to review your motives for action. Review the activities in your Momentum Journal and clarify "What you want to be known for."

Next, schedule time with a mentor, someone you can meet for a coffee, a lunch, or a long walk-n-talk. Let them know what you're challenged by, and get some ideas and advice from them.

Create a smaller, new, interim milestone. Look out 30 days and commit to having completed some subproject that will indicate you're making progress.

Once you have a milestone, choose what you'll monitor to make sure you're on course to achieve that goal. Or, what you'll notice to indicate you're "running on empty" and need to ask for help or rewrite the goal you're trying to achieve.

Jason's Momentum Experience

In January 2013, I facilitated a month-long, online coaching program called *Achieve Your Next* for 11 executives from companies across America. This Executive Coaching program provided the opportunity for clients to create and commit to new and better workflow processes while learning new routines to achieve their annual professional and personal goals.

On Monday of each week, I e-mailed them a worksheet with specific workplace performance, productivity, and time management skills to practice. On Wednesday, I presented a 45-minute Master Class webinar, outlining the specifics of the tactics and answering any questions. Then, on Thursday and Friday, I scheduled one-on-one meetings with each client. The goal was to personalize their own personal/professional productivity plan (PPPP) for the rest of the year.

At the end of the course, every person said that they practiced new behaviors, learned new techniques, and felt more prepared to take on their yearly objectives. Out of the 11 people I talked to at the close of the program, eight of them used the word *momentum*. They said things like:

"Now that I've got *momentum*, how do I keep it?"

"I feel like I've got *momentum* and hope it stays."

"When I'm working with these techniques, I have *momentum*."

Hearing this feedback gave me the insight and the idea to modify that program into something different. Ultimately, it is what inspired Jodi and I to cofound the Get Momentum Leadership Academy, a membership program that helps leaders empower themselves by learning 12 leadership skills required to be influential and gain the knowledge, confidence, and experience needed to face today's evolving business challenges.

But, Change Isn't Easy

Change presents challenges, and you probably have some great reasons to avoid it!

According to research published by Harvard professor Rosabeth Moss Kanter, chair and director of the Harvard Advanced Leadership Initiative, there are several reasons to put off modifying what you do and how you do things.

When you think about what you'd like to be doing differently, how many of these sound familiar?

1. **More work.** If you *do* make changes, you'll just get more to do!
2. **Surprises.** You don't know what *might* happen if you do things differently.
3. **Uncertainty.** You aren't sure if things will work out or really be any better.
4. **Loss of control.** On some level, a willingness to do things differently means you might not have known everything before and might not have all the answers!

These are valid concerns. But, they're not insurmountable barriers. You can handle a little uncertainty and extra work for the sake of your dream, right?

Will it be easy? Maybe. Maybe not. Will it be worthwhile? Absolutely!

Why It's Hard to Get Momentum

It's comfortable to hold on to old habits and keep doing what used to work. Change is hard.

We know; we have been there. In 1995, Jason considered spending another four years at university when he was invited to pursue a doctoral degree in education. By the middle of 2006, Jodi knew she had stayed in an administrative job more than a year after she knew it was time to move on.

Right now, you have really, *really* good reasons not to change the way you do your life. To begin with, it's just more comfortable to hold on to what you used to do. We want to believe that what we know should work, even when it doesn't.

Which of the following scenarios do you relate to most?

1. I Can't Admit That I'm Wrong

How many times have you held on to a position—maybe while arguing with a partner or in a heated discussion with an upset customer—long after you realized that you were indeed wrong? In many cases, modifying your position—no matter how small or significant—means you have to admit that you didn't know the best way to do it. You're admitting that you were wrong at some level, and nobody likes to do that.

2. Change Is Expensive; I Can't Afford It

Yes, it costs to change. Sometimes it costs a lot! And, it's completely possible the most expensive part of making a change is looking back on what you were trying to do, realizing you spent a lot of money doing it, and walking away. While it is an expensive lesson to learn, in the long term, you'll look back and be proud that you had the confidence to trust yourself and make the change you knew was right.

3. Change Is Time-Consuming. Another Cost!

Like money, you might have spent a lot of time trying to start that project or make that change. Here, it's easy to reflect on how much of your life—late nights, weekends, cancelled vacations, and so on—you may have given to what you hoped would work out.

4. I Tried to Change. It Doesn't Last.

Some people are so willing to change that they never stick with anything long enough to see it all the way through. If you're like a lot of people we meet with, you've tried to get momentum. You've downloaded apps; implemented time management programs; bought into a productivity system; joined numerous social, athletic, or alumni associations; and have even gone to conferences. You tried a little bit of a lot, hoping that the next thing you try will be *the* thing that will make a difference.

An Outsider's Perspective

When and where possible, get expert advice. Experts study what you're trying to do for a living. You can e-mail them, call them, or even meet them for coffee or lunch in your down time. This is a great way to find out if what you're doing is going to help you get to where you want to go. When possible, ask an outsider (a friend, a mentor, a coach) to observe what you're doing and the way you're doing it. You will be amazed what you learn from someone else's perspective.

Jason's Momentum Experience

I've been facilitating workshops for more than 20 years. Every slide deck I create includes short embedded video clips. I add 30 second to 2:00 minute-long videos to showcase a point or to introduce a concept. However, it wasn't always this way. Before, it was very difficult to show these video clips. I arrived to the client site up to two hours before the scheduled start time. I logged on to the Internet (very difficult in some of the highly secure buildings I work in) and organized web browser tabs with each video I was going to show. Sometimes the site was blocked, and I needed an on-site administrator from the IT department to help me get through their firewall!

During the presentation, when it came time to show a particular clip, I stopped the presentation, switched to the web browser, went to the video site, and clicked the "play" button there. I knew it was distracting, but I considered that to be the cost of the activity.

One day in 2008, I invited one of my coaches to observe me present a local program in Ventura, California. I wanted her to assess my facilitation skills looking for a specific area for improvement. She found the opportunity right away!

After the program was done, we sat down for a coffee to go through the four-hour-long presentation. She immediately told me how distracting it was each of the three times I stopped the workshop to show video clips. Although she thought the videos were powerful, she felt their value was being overshadowed by the confusion of me "fooling with my computer and the Internet."

I hired a digital editor for three hours to teach me how to download video clips from the Internet, edit the parts I wanted to show, and then embed those clips into my presentation. Instantly, I transformed the way I presented my slide decks. Did I have to come to terms with the fact that in more than 800 seminars over the previous nine years I had been distracting my audiences? Yes. Did it take some time and money to learn how to do this? Yes. Did I need to learn a new way of doing things? Yes.

Was it worth it? Absolutely! Over and over again, people in my programs comment on the seamlessness between audio, video, and storytelling in my programs. That video training cost me a couple hundred bucks, but it was time and money well spent. This investment in my continual professional improvement has paid for itself over and over again.

Modifying Isn't Failing

Just because you're making a change doesn't mean something is wrong with you. Because you want to do better doesn't mean you or your project is broken. Look around at where you are. Life is good, you're breathing right? Work is okay, right? Your current knowledge and practices got you where you are. Acknowledge yourself for the effort you've made and the success you've achieved that led you to this point.

You've put yourself out there; you've made the effort. Now it's time to take it all to the next level.

Basketball legend Michael Jordan said it best: "I've missed more than 9,000 shots in my career. I've lost almost 300 games. Twenty-six times, I've been trusted to take the game-winning shot and missed. I've failed over and over and over again in my life and that is why I succeed."

Jodi's Momentum Experience

In September 2014, I started to think, "It's time to change." Changing was hard for all the reasons we've just shared with you, but most of all for me, it was the self-judgment that I had been wasting my time for years.

After hosting Women's Business Socials every month for almost five years, the last three months were just good, not great. I was comfortable with the results (80 to 100 businesswomen attended each month), but I knew my heart wasn't in it anymore.

I felt *done* with the whole experience. I wanted to do more than gather women to talk; I wanted to coach them to create improvements in their companies.

By the middle of 2014, I decided the Get Momentum Leadership Academy was what I wanted to put my time, energy, and focus into growing. I stopped producing the Women's Business Socials.

So, I took all of that experience and information and applied it to Get Momentum. I've found ways to apply what I learned over the years to make this a vibrant community.

Still Struggling with Change?

If you're still struggling with making a change, maybe you're too close to the problem. Perhaps you've spent too much time thinking about what or how to change. Our advice, which may seem counterintuitive, is this: Step away.

Or ride away, walk away, play away, get away. We know that when you're under pressure to perform, the last thing you'll think of doing is taking a break! But, the mental pause you give yourself by getting away could be just what you need. You'll see things from a new perspective and come back to the project refreshed.

Not changing may be causing some of the most difficult and painful experiences of being stuck in your project because change is all about self-reflection. In order to make a change, you need to know yourself, your legacy, and your overall goal.

GET MOMENTUM ACTIVITY #23: What One Change Can I Make to Move Forward?

Spend some time thinking about the Momentum Question: "What one change can I make to keep moving forward?"

As you modify (make small changes), keep these two questions in mind:

1. What should I do more of?
2. What should I do less of?

+1 Productivity versus 2x Productivity

We know you're busy. No doubt your schedule is full every day. Maybe you're double-booked with meetings before you even arrive to work. And your personal life is stressful as you think about everything that's still undone.

When you're overwhelmed with a backlog to do, you are in a position to make a decision:

1. Work another hour each day to catch up. We call this +1 Productivity.

   OR

2. Study how to work to be twice as efficient. We call this 2x Productivity.

Working Harder and Longer

Everybody starts with +1 Productivity because it's easy to do—at first. You go into work an hour early when it's quiet or stay an hour later after everyone else has left. Then you add another hour (+1) after dinner to just check e-mail "really quickly." Pretty soon, you're working on Sunday afternoon (+1) so you're not surprised by anything on Monday morning. Does this sound familiar?

The problem with +1 Productivity is that eventually, you run out of hours to add! You feel like you're working all the time. You never really get away from it. And the worst part is that it doesn't have any lasting effect.

Catching up this weekend probably won't eliminate the need to do it again next weekend. It's time to work smarter.

Improving How You Work

So now it's time to make a big investment in yourself. You're going to need to learn something new and possibly spend a bit of time setting up new systems. Apply 2x Productivity techniques to your workflow. We'll show you how.

Once you start working this way, you'll be more efficient and will recoup the time invested many times over. If you save just 15 minutes a week by running one meeting more efficiently, you'll save an additional 12 hours a year. If you figure out a way to save five minutes a day in how you process your e-mail, for example, that gives you back almost 21 hours a year. Outsource even some of the errands you run each month, and you could save another 25 hours a year.

Here's an example: Jodi used to go to the bank about twice each week to deposit checks. Each trip took her about 15 minutes. On the surface, no big deal. On an annual basis, it meant she was out of the office about 25 hours a year…during peak business times! But, once she started using the banking check deposit app on her phone, she regained that time. What did she fill that time with? Ask her and she'll tell you. Some days it meant she got to go for a walk with our dog, Zuma. Other days she went to lunch with a mentor. Investing in figuring out how to 2x your productivity might give you the time you say you need.

What are you waiting for? Ready to give the 2x Productivity process a chance?

Focus on *One* Change

While it is tempting to consider changing several things all at once, our coaching advice is always going to be: Choose less, more.

That is, focus on *one* change to make, and focus on that one change as much as possible. Consider the following categories and think about focusing on one of them to change.

1. The Goal
2. The Information
3. The Process

As an example, suppose you were training to complete a marathon and you were not meeting your milestones, such as the total number of miles run per week. You could consider one of the following areas to focus on and modify.

1. *The Goal*: You could decide not to run the marathon or to reschedule for a later race.
2. *The Information*: You could sign up for a running clinic or connect with a running coach to acquire new information.
3. *The Process*: You could change your schedule of long runs to midweek if you're not doing them on the weekend. You could also run with a new group or run at a different time of day than you were before.

Let's dive deeper into each of those areas that you could change.

1. The Goal

Do I want to modify my overall goal?

Within a month or three of working on your project, you'll have a great idea of how far along you've come. You'll know what is working and what is not.

The more clear you are on the "what," the more committed you may feel to working on that project. However, if you're struggling to make even basic progress, it may be time to reconsider the goal you're working to achieve. We're not suggesting you abandon it, and we aren't coaching you to rethink everything. We simply want you to ask yourself, "Can I focus on a smaller piece of the project I had in mind? Can I work to achieve a significant aspect of that original project that—when completed—will put me on track to take on bigger milestones of that overall project?"

It's important to note two things about modifying your goal:

1. You're not giving up. In fact, when you modify the next three months of goals, you may find that you wind up making *more* progress than before, just because you're taking small, consistent actions, unlike before, when you were stuck.

2. You're not stopping. Indeed, starting small often builds momentum because you'll be able to complete the smaller objectives. It feels good to finish something. And that gives you confidence to take on the next level.

2. The Information

Do I modify what I know or think?

Everything you know has gotten you this far. Acknowledge that and congratulate yourself. But—and this is important—if you're going to keep your project moving forward, you're surely going to have to learn something new.

To gain new information, look at the books on your shelves, the magazines on your desk, the bookmarked websites on your web browser. If you're going to *do* something new, *learn* something new.

You should also look at your social circles. Who you're hanging out with at the end of the day has a big impact on whether you talk about what's possible or listen to people complain. If your goal is to launch a business, ask yourself if you're hanging out with people who have started businesses. If you're not, why not? Find out where these folks meet up and join them.

3. The Process

Do I modify how I'm doing what I'm doing?

In order to make a change, you need to do things *differently*. You have to start looking at what work you can (1) automate, (2) delegate, or (3) eliminate. Here are some examples.

1. Automate: Convert a Process to a Largely Automatic Operation

The easiest way to start automating tasks is to understand what you do automatically. Maybe you've never considered alternatives to going to the grocery store or paying bills or sending the same e-mail over and over to different people. Once you start looking for things to automate in your personal and professional life, you'll start noticing solutions that may save you minutes to hours in your day, every day.

Jason and Jodi's examples of automation:

- We automated our banking using online bill pay.
- We automated the purchase and receipt of our household and office supplies using Amazon Subscribe.
- We automated our e-mail delivery to people requesting information from our website.

2. Delegate: Entrust a Task or Responsibility to Another Person

We've all said it: "It'll be easier if I just do it." And usually this is true. It's faster and easier in that moment, but this strategy is from the +1 Productivity mindset. When you train your team (coworkers, staff, family members, etc.) to take on a task that needs to be done, but not necessarily by you, then you're implementing 2x Productivity.

Jason and Jodi's examples of delegation:

- We delegated the production and publishing of Jason's podcast to a freelancer.
- We delegated website maintenance to a development team and recently expanded their role to managing all tech updates and several other administrative technical tasks.
- We delegated our landscaping work to a gardener to do all the "heavy lifting" of cleaning up and maintenance for the garden so that we get to do more of the fun activities in the garden that bring us joy.

3. Eliminate: Completely Remove or Get Rid of Something

Why get rid of some habits and routines? Well, you're busy, right? You already have too much to do, and you probably don't have enough time to add anything new. So often, we hear our colleagues, friends, and even family say that they just have too much to do. And, because of that, they can't get to that project they want to start.

As mentioned earlier, one of Jason's mentors, Marshall Goldsmith, wrote a great book titled *What Got You Here Won't Get You There*. There, Marshall describes the habits and routines of high-level managers inside some of the world's largest companies and how they realized they had to eliminate certain work if they were going to reach their next level of success.

Think about this very carefully. If you can't get to what you want to do because you're already busy doing the things you're busy doing, there is only one solution: Stop doing some of those things!

Jason and Jodi's examples of eliminated tasks:

- We eliminated trips to the bank to deposit checks by using a bank app for all deposits.
- We eliminated unnecessary meetings. (Review the meetings you're invited to. Decline meetings that are not keeping you on course and certainly the ones that conflict with you working on your most important projects.)
- We eliminated obligations and guilt-induced agreements. Identify any priorities you are making more important than your own. Go back to the first Momentum Question: "What do you want to be known for?" Let your answer be your guide.

GET MOMENTUM ACTIVITY #24: Modifying in Practice

Increase your awareness of the work you do, and especially the work you have that isn't getting done on time (or at all!). Use your Momentum Journal to list what tasks you can automate, delegate, or eliminate. If you don't know where to start, contact your mentor (see Chapter 4) or review the next 90 days of milestones.

(continued)

(*continued*)

You can also make a list of activities that feel like a waste of time.

While we know it is tempting to make big changes all at once, over the years, we have learned that the best way to sustain momentum is to completely install one small modification at a time. Focus on changing one thing, and then going on to something else. In this chapter, we give you three specific kinds of small changes you can make: automate, delegate, or eliminate.

Every month or so, we question the routines we do and ask ourselves if we could possibly set up a system or a process to do it in less time than it currently takes.

You can't sustain +1 Productivity if you're already maxed out, and you're already pushing up against the clock every morning and every evening. Choose your changes wisely, and implement the ones that will help you get momentum.

Sustain the Change

Do you know someone who would help you stay accountable to your commitments and new behaviors? Having an accountability partner as well as a deadline, like a monthly check-in, will help you stay on track and sustain the changes you make.

If the changes you make are not sustainable, what's the point? Sure you can pull all-nighters to make a deadline, but living due date to due date is no way to get ahead. And, it's certainly not a way to build a career or long-term relationships. At this final stage of momentum, use everything you've learned about how to focus on the changes you want to make and implement specific strategies to multiply the impact of your own productivity.

To Do and Share

1. Change is not easy, but it is well worth the effort. Review what you monitored in Chapter 6 to guide what to modify. Making one change can mean the difference in completing your project or not.
2. Replace +1 Productivity with 2x Productivity to gain more time! Making micro-changes to how you work will have a more lasting impact than just working more hours.
3. Make *one* change at a time. Decide if you're going to change your goal, the information you collect, or the process of your workflow. Remember to focus on multiplying your productivity by automating, delegating, or eliminating work.

What Comes Next

You now have the strategies, tools, and mindset for starting anything that was stuck. In the next chapter, learn how to share the empowering process of Get Momentum that you've experienced with the people you spend so much time with at work, at home, and in your community.

8

You Did It!

Focus on Impact

One chilly California morning in December of 2015, Jason facilitated a leadership workshop for a small group of senior leaders at a social media company in Silicon Valley. A few weeks prior to the event, he reviewed the five core values of the organization. Each statement was designed to provide employees and visitors alike with a clear mission, vision, and direction of what leadership in that company believes is important.

The first core value on the list, "Focus on impact," reminded Jason of the Stage 1 Motivation Question: "What do you want to be known for?" During his time on campus with employees from various departments in the organization, he asked people what that first value meant to them. Over and over again, it was a reminder that regardless of how that question is phrased, the key to momentum is to connect to the reason why you do what you do.

As your coaches, we want you to identify—and identify with—your purpose. We want you to know what's important to you, and why. We believe the most important thing you can focus on is the impact your actions, choices, and achievements have on your life and the lives of the people you care about.

To achieve your potential, you need to answer the legacy question and determine the positive and constructive impact you'll have on those you serve throughout your life.

Get Momentum in Life and at Work

By now, you know that getting momentum isn't something you do just once. And you know that it applies to more than just a stuck project at work. Indeed, the answers to all five Momentum Questions apply as much to your life as they do to your work.

As you think about being, living, and working at your best, consider some unique capabilities you possess such as:

Clear Your Mind

When you're stressed and under pressure to perform, take out a blank piece of paper and write down 50 (or more) things that are on your mind. When each thing you think about "has a piece of you," it's hard to focus on what motivates you. Review the list and decide what you'll focus on... and what you can ignore for now.

Practice Asking for Help

We're smarter together.... We know that about ourselves, and by now we hope you feel that way, too. When we ask for help it isn't a sign of weakness; it is in fact a demonstration of strength. By raising your hand, stating what it is you need help with, and talking with people who care about your success, you increase the likelihood that you'll achieve your goals.

Look into the Future

Use the future to pull yourself out of what's stressing you now. As you look out beyond what is due this week and see what's coming toward you, start to organize yourself to take full advantage of the opportunities coming your way. Sure, you have a lot to catch up on, that's why it is so important you start working today on those things that are due 30 (or more) days from now.

Increase Your Awareness

Know what you're looking for so that when you see it—even if it's subtle—you'll notice it. Your mind grows as you notice things, and if you want it to grow in positive ways, look for positive things. Keep your mental radar on. The more you notice, the more you'll notice! Keep finding examples of the things that give you energy.

Make Small Changes, Consciously

Not everything, not all at once. Now that you've gotten started, keep the momentum you have by implementing small changes, one at a time. You can sustain this style of change over time. Cultivate the discipline to find out what you need to do, and to do what you know you need!

In each city we visit, each workshop we facilitate, and every Get Momentum Leadership Retreat we host, Get Momentum members say that their momentum doesn't stop at the end of their project. As they answer the five Momentum Questions at work, their home life improves. And when they apply the Momentum Questions to their home life, their work challenges become easier.

People used to talk about achieving some kind of work-life balance. It was almost as though they were separating the complexities of each into distinct parts of themselves that had to be managed and controlled differently. Now, however, they find that life and work are connected. The leader they want to be known as at work is not unlike the person they want to be known as at home. They want to be:

- Trustworthy
- Committed

- Kind
- Generous
- Supportive
- Productive

Let yourself apply what you know about managing yourself and managing projects to both the professional and the personal projects you're committed to.

Practice the five-stage Get Momentum process. The next time your child scores low on an exam or your partner lets you down by not doing what he or she promised, you have the chance to ask yourself, "What do I want to be known for?" The power of a well-placed question is that it acts as a pattern-interrupt; by the time you finish answering that first Momentum Question, you could find the pressure lessening, your heart rate slowing, and your response time lengthening. And you could find yourself responding in a more positive and constructive way to the situations around you.

A Life of No Regrets

We mentioned Bronnie Ware's book *The Top Five Regrets of the Dying* in Chapter 1. As you reread each regret listed, take a moment and reflect on how asking the five Momentum Questions can prevent you from experiencing these regrets.

1. I wish I'd had the courage to live a life true to myself, not the life others expected of me.
2. I wish I hadn't worked so hard.
3. I wish I'd had the courage to express my feelings.
4. I wish I had stayed in touch with my friends.
5. I wish that I had let myself be happier.

The Get Momentum process gives you the tools to live a life true to yourself and make the impact you're here to make.

Momentum, Self-Reflection, and Self-Confidence

During one of our #CoffeeChat events at a favorite bakery in Marin County, the president of a document management services firm said, "The work you two do…it's really about getting people to do more self-reflection, isn't it? I understand. We don't get enough time to think about who we are and why we do the things we do."

The more you practice applying the Momentum Stages and Questions to your life and work, the more natural it will be to think this way. Building momentum, achieving outcomes, and taking time to reflect on your progress is a way to build self-confidence. In doing so, you increase your willingness to take on ever greater levels of responsibility, accountability, and contribution.

Yoda said, "For my ally is the Force. And a powerful ally it is. Life creates it, makes it grow. Its energy surrounds us and binds us."

This is how we feel about our Get Momentum process.

The Best Way to Learn It Is to Teach It

Oh, and one more thing…

Just because you've done the self-reflective work we've coached you to complete doesn't mean everyone else has. The more times you apply the Momentum Questions to projects as needed, the more natural it's going to be to want to share this information and this process with those around you.

Imagine if when your department directors sat down in a meeting, everyone in the room knew what they wanted to be known for. Wouldn't it be easier to support each other? Wouldn't it help you all continue to grow and develop as leaders who are contributing to the organization's overall mission?

Now, think about whom you can share the Get Momentum process with in your life or at your work.

Where to Go from Here

When we started our coaching firm back in 2007, our mantra was "We're smarter and better together." We said it about every project we took on, every client we served, and every book proposal we submitted.

Throughout this journey, you have had the opportunity to come along with us. We hope that as a result, you completed, or are well on your way to completing, your big project. We hope that you have momentum.

Whatever you need, we're just a click away.

Leave us a note at www.GetMomentum.com/book

Jodi and Jason Womack

Resources to Help You Keep the Momentum You've Started

THIS ISN'T THE END; IT'S just the beginning. Here are three ways to stay connected to the power of Get Momentum.

1. **Visit the *Get Momentum* book website.**

   Download a PDF workbook of all the Get Momentum Activities and Journal prompts. You can also watch videos and take the Get Momentum Quiz. Sign up to receive the free Get Momentum e-mails we send from time to time. And, be sure to send us a note! We'd love to hear from you.

   www.GetMomentum.com/book

2. **Join the Get Momentum Leadership Academy.**

   You've had a taste of what we're like as coaches and accountability partners. If you're ready to join us and experience the support, interaction, and community, choose the membership level of the Get Momentum Leadership Academy that matches your interest and budget.

   www.GetMomentum.com

3. Bring the Get Momentum Workshop to your next company event.

Get Momentum Workshops are the easiest—and fastest—way to ready your team or your entire organization to improve professional skills and personal abilities. Imagine when your whole team is prepared to achieve their most important goals.

These one- to three-day workshops are not the "rah-rah" kind of motivation of yesteryear, but authentic experiences that bring people together and give them something positive to talk about for months, if not years.

The easiest and fastest way to Get Momentum at work is to share the experience. Invite the Womacks to personally guide you and your team as you work together to:

- Identify your purpose as an organization. Start with "why."
- Create a plan to make progress on your goals and implement a structured accountability system to keep you on course.
- Use the strategies you read and practiced here in the book on your real projects, both at work and at home.

Visit www.GetMomentum.com/workshop for all the details and sign up for more information.

Thank You

OUR TEAM AT WILEY:

Matt Holt, Peter Knox, Lia Ottaviano, Barbara Long, Caroline Maria Vincent.

To our friends who've been there for us, always dealing with our last-minute schedule changes. Yeah, we fly a lot...

Alejandra Abella de Aristegui, Alexis Ridenour, Bert Mahoney, Clemens Wan, Dave Hackel, Debbie Godfrey, Dyana Valentine, Jacqui Burge, James Ellengold, Jennifer Bezoza, Joe Bruzzese, Jon Furness, Kara DeFrias, Kathryn Cox, Keren Taylor, Kira Ryder, Liz Harward, Lynda Polk, Melody Biringer, Quanah Ridenour, Rick Kantor, Shelley Shoemaker, Torry Burdick.

We wouldn't be here without our mentors and teachers. You keep us on our toes, and teach us every day.

Ali Brown, Andrew DeCurtis, Brett Laymance, Carol Kline, Chris Brogan, Dwayne Melançon, Frances Hesselbein, Jim Polk, Keith Ferrazzi, Kevin Wilde, Larry Chambers, Mark Biallas, Martin Jones, Mary Dean, Pam Slim, Pip Coburn, Rajesh Setty, Rao Machiraju, Seth Godin, Steve Silverman.

And, our professional colleagues. You pick up the phone when we call, and we thank you every day for that.

Bill DeMarco, Christine Boccieri, Christopher Knapp, David Deacon, David Bailey, David Vik, Frank Buck, Gary Ware, Gregg Faceglia, Hamish Macqueen, Harold Wimberly, Japjot Sethi, Jennifer Rotker, Jon Peters, Josh Linkner, Kevin DeNoia, Kirn Pakal, Kirsten Giles, Kristi Ling, Kymberlee Weil, Laura Stack, Lisa Macqueen, Lorri Friefeld, Marc Effron, Mark Sylvester, Marlo Scott, Michael Butler, Michel Koopman, Miriam Ort, Peter Mahoney, Ramon Ray, Randy Harward, Ravi Gundlapalli, Richie Norton, Rob Bernshteyn, Rob Greer, Ron Bezoza, Ron Garrow, Sarah Childers, Shawn Ramsingh, Steinar Hjelle, Steve Harden, Tanya Macaluso, Tim Braheem, Tim O'Keefe, Tina Morgan, Tom Catalini, Tony Ubertaccio, Vishal Bhatia.

To Jason's Family… We did it, again!

Craig and Gail Womack; Nancy Martinez, Felice Martinez, and Nate Womack.

To Jodi's Big Crazy Family, I love, love, love you…

Jim and Eileen Rosenthal; Heidi, Ross, Ethan and Carly!

And again…thank you to the founding Get Momentum Members:

Alex Caragiannides, Allison Taylor, Alton Harris, Amy Graham, Andrea Aresca, Ant Polglase, Ariana Friedlander, Art Carden, Bilal Loya, Bocar Kane, Brad Wasserman, Brian McRae, Bridgett Bolden, Bruce Menke, Catherine Meyer, Chris McCauley, Christi Harris, Cico Rodriguez, Dan Lloyd, Danielle Beal, Darrel Weaver, David Schneider, Devon Bandison, Dianne Digianantonio, Domenic Bruzzese, Dwayne Melancon, Edgar Gil Rizzatti, Eric Hubbard, Erica O'Toole, Erin Newkirk, Fabien Modoux, Fazia Merhai, Felice Martinez, Geoffrey Grow, Geoffrey Pfeifer, Gil Ouellette, Ifeanyi Enoch Onuoha, Inez Gonzalez, Ivor Subotic, Jackie Compton, Jacob Fulton, Jason Peterson, Jason Thompson, Jen Speed, Jenna Fleur, Jeremiah Wean, Joe Drago, Joel Pastore, Jonathon McIntyre, Judith Sawitsky, Jun Villa, Justin Gaetano, Kapil Apshankar, Katherine Lutz, Kay Woodard, Keith Mitchum, Khedra Mathis, Kirsten Giles, Kris Huggins, Kristi

Palma, Kyle Tanner, Larry Perlov, Leia Parker, Maggie Musser, Marc Avery, Marc Pitcher, Marie-Claire Hermans, Mark Jackson, Mark McArthur, Mark Rosky, Mark Weingartner, Martine Mathewson, Matthew Cousins, Max Reed, Maxime Charron, Melissa DeWeese, Michael Walsh, Mohammad Rahman, Mozart Guerrier, Mufaro Nyachoto, Nancy Earle, Natalie Houston, Nick Lascelles, Nicole Anthony, Nikolas Chapapas, Noah Ewing, Pat Friel, Paul Gierow, Phil Stanoch, Rachel Bodnar, Rachel Von Hendrix, Ranjani Mohana, Ravi Gundlapalli, Rob Bremmer, Robb Zarges, Robert Freeman, Roberta Raye, Roger Carr, Rohan Handa, Roylin Downs, Ryan Morris, Ryan Speed, Scott Kuhn, Scott Moskowitz, Shayla Higginbotham, Stacey Wong, Stephen Paine, Steve Harden, Steven Manuel, Summer McGinnis, Sumukh Setty, Susan Bardsley, Susan Johnson, Tamarind Rossetti, Tara Roberts, Tim Huebsch, Tina Baugh, Tom Froelich, Tom Klein, Tony Ubertaccio, Venkatesh Iyer, Vernon Foster II, Virginia Bahadkar, Walter Hartford, Will Gandy.

Index